THE END OF EVERYTHING

A society in transition

THE END OF EVERYTHING

A society in transition

ADRIÁN GORDALIZA VEGA

THE END OF EVERYTHING
A society in transition
© 2023 Adrián Gordaliza Vega

Cover: Adrián Gordaliza Vega

Layout: www.jgarridomaquetacion.com

© Premium Languages

*Thanks to Ben Smith for being
the indirect instigator of this book*

CONTENTS

PREFACE

During the first months of the lockdown that followed the COVID-19 outbreak, one of my students suggested the possibility of looking at the situation that we were experiencing from a philosophical perspective. In order to provide some context we decided to start with a basic course in the History of Philosophy covering from the origins of Philosophy in ancient Greece to the beginning of the 21st century.

Although interesting, the classes and the notes that I prepared were too academic and failed to convey the true potential that Philosophy can have when it is applied to other aspects of everyday life.

It was then that we decided to hold sessions dedicated to discussing current issues that are common currency in our society. It was no longer a question of seeing the differences between Descartes and Kant, but of applying philosophical concepts to topics such as contemporary politics, the problems derived from the debate on climate change, the issue of transsexuals and their conflict with feminism, the controversy over vaccines, identity politics, the popularity of veganism, dating apps, etc.

This was the real genesis of the book, the revelation that reality is much more complex than it seems and that it is always in transformation; always in conflict. We need to accept that some ideas oppose others and in many cases we have to take sides. Philosophical analysis helps in the elaboration of an opinion and the formation of a critical conscience; something that is essential today if we want to understand what is happening around us.

Obviously, the issues discussed here do not have a universal vocation. They are circumscribed to a time (the 21st century) and a space (more or less that of Western societies). However, these are a good number of issues in constant flux of our reality. Furthermore, the only advice I would allow myself to give the reader is: flee from those ideologies with a universal vocation that treat all individuals and societies in the same way.

It was at this point that I started writing a book about you and I. About our neighbours, our partners, our families, our friends, our co-workers and most of the people we know.

Four themes constantly run through the book: dialectical changes, power struggles, sex and death. However, these topics necessarily link with some others such as politics, medicine, climate change, art or social media.

Despite the density of the topics covered, this is not intended to be a boring book. Throughout the following chapters you will be introduced to adulterous presidents, jilted lovers, homophobes turned into transexuals, artists who smear themselves with excrement, racist scientists, suicidal musicians, successful alchemists, vengeful goddesses, philosophers sentenced to death and a long etcetera of captivating characters that paradoxically will help us in forming a better idea of our society and its links with the past.

INTRODUCTION

We live in a world where there is
more and more information
and less and less meaning
(Jean Baudrillard)

About society

The society of which we all form a part is much more than the sum of its individuals. It shapes the way we think or act. The aim with this book is to show how our ideas regarding love, democracy, nature, animals, death and many others are not static or monolithic. They evolve over time, and change depending on the place in which we live.

These changes are massive and have deeply altered our way of understanding things and the way we relate to others. These transformations are not merely an intellectual trend, they also have a practical dimension that is easy to observe in our daily lives. On these pages we will be dealing with the profound shift in our attitude regarding relationships, consumption, education, fashion, tastes, values, etc.

The rapid accumulation of cultural mutations in recent decades (roughly speaking after the Second World War) justifies the need to talk about a new social order; one that has been called in different ways: post-modernism, post-industrial society, late capitalism or neoliberalism. Each one of these terms have its own connotations, but they all refer to an evolutionary state of transition between an era known as 'modern age' and a society with enough peculiar features to be considered something different (let us call it 'post-modern'). What these changes are, how they affect us and what philosophical root we can identify in them, is the subject of this book.

Any individual is born within the context of a society. We all are members of one, although sometimes it could be more than only one. Depending on the case, that society can be very small, for example a tribe in the Amazon. In other instances, individuals are part of a much larger society, for example someone born in France or in China. Right from the beginning, the individual members are an active part (not merely passive) of a society that 'transfers' to them a language, traditions, values, beliefs, social status, etc. As a whole, they form an arsenal of adaptive tools to the environment in which a certain group evolves.

Using a technological analogy of our time, they are like applications in a mobile phone that are necessary to communicate with one another and our surroundings. In the most developed societies there are institutions such as schools, churches, social media or universities that are responsible for disseminating these contents to individuals. They have the last word in considering what is legal, what is acceptable, what is normal or what is beautiful. To continue with the analogy, individuals are not born with these applications, we download them from these institutions. However, as in real life, not all applications are compatible and sometimes we need to upgrade our operative system. If we keep thinking as if we're in in 1995 we will have a hard time understanding the world today. What may have been acceptable a decade ago might be completely unacceptable today. In the same way, we can still make a phone call from a phone made in the 90s but we are going to miss a lot of things.

Traditionally, our knowledge, values and beliefs have been very similar for parents and children. Obviously, there are also some changes between generations, but usually they are gradual and tend to be slow. The positive aspect of this is that they provide a sense of unity and continuity between the members of any given society. However, the changes that we have experienced during the last decades are so numerous, so deep, so radical in their substance and in their form that they have destabilised the previous unity and continuity. Where there was harmony and balance, today there is fragmentation. The old order has been shattered and our society is increasingly more fragmented creating the perfect condition for new niches to appear. Anyone working in marketing today knows that very well. You do not advertise to everyone, everything is segmented in niches of interest, class, education, nationality, etc.

Author's intention

However, the fragmentation we are describing necessarily generates conflict among certain groups. This antagonism is manifested in cultural wars, identity politics, 'wokism', derogatory comments on social media, extreme political parties, etc. The repercussions are many and this book tries to make sense of all that.

Although at first it may seem that these constant changes in the foundation of Western societies are random or capricious, in fact there is a rational evolutionary line that unfolds historically. At least, we can point to the intellectual 'epicenters' that have introduced some of those changes which makes us be who we are and think the way we do.

I have written this book with intellectual premise that everything that is currently happening in our Western societies is also rational. There must be a reason for today's changes and my intention is to explore that. If today's teenagers consider themselves to be 'gender fluid', it is not only to shock their parents and teachers (although this should not be ruled out). If contemporary art confuses museum visitors, it is not because artists want to feel misunderstood (although this should not be ruled out). If the working class is voting for extreme right-wing political parties, it is not because they are all ignorant racists (although some are). If there are intellectuals who question that democracy is the best political system, it is not because they want to establish a fascist or communist dictatorship (although some would be delighted).

With the limitation of my means (material and intellectual), I hope that I succeeded in being entertaining without falling into purely academic discussions. At the same time, the chapters are full of references to Plato, Hegel or Derrida, not with the intention of showing scholarship but to further support my arguments.

If there is an ultimate motivation that I seek with the following pages, it would be to provide a guide, an intellectual compass, that could be helpful navigating the changes that we have to live through (and that on many occasions do not seem to be purely rational or make any sense). Do not try to read this book in the hope of finding a spiritual balm, or a cure for the diseases of the 'soul' of the 21st century, instead you will find a diagnosis of what it means to be a citizen of our western societies today.

The thesis of this book is that we are immerse in a massive shift between a modern society and a post-modern one. It is very difficult to say when this movement really started but the Second World War is clearly a referent as it is all the events around 1968, the counter-culture and decolonisation of many countries.

Modernity on the other hand, strove to classify. Modern philosophers and scientists tried to order and define the world. It was an incessant work of labelling 'the reality'. Post-modernity, on the other hand, would want to remove the labels. All of them.

This is the new world we live in. It is almost impossible to be neutral in considering these hot topics, however much we try. For my part, I have not pretended to be so in this book.

Quick overview of the book

I open the book arguing that we live in a society that is in transition (although that can be said of many others). Ours is a society that is no longer modern, as it used to be, but also not completely post-modern (if it ever could be). I analyse the defining features of Western society halfway between yesterday and tomorrow, and how that affects our daily lives.

In the second chapter, I deal with truths, lies, and anything in between. I examine the rise of 'fake news' and the use of concepts such as 'post-truth', 'post-factual' or 'narratives'. The chapter deals with the constant questioning of 'big truths' in contemporary society and how certain powers build their own truths around their interests.

In the third chapter, I question whether democracy is the most elevated political system that has ever been (or will ever exist). We will be asking very uncomfortable questions like: 'Is democracy an untouchable ideology as a religious dogma?' or 'Is it even legitimate to question some of the aspects of the democratic system?'.

The fourth chapter is dedicated to considering some of the most relevant positions in the debate about climate change. Again, there will be some controversial issues here, but ones that need to be addressed if we want to fully explore our reality.

In the fifth chapter, I deal with contemporary post-modern art and why it is so difficult for many people to accept it. I will show that contemporary art is not just a joke (at least not all the time), although humour also plays an important part in it. I will give a more accurate definition of what 'art' means today in order to include the new expressive forms of contemporary art.

Our relationship with animals forms the bulk of the sixth chapter. I consider the status of animals with regards to humans. Are we at the same level, or are we different? I analyse some aspects of vegetarianism, veganism and the controversial arguments of the so called 'most dangerous philosopher in the world', Peter Singer.

With the seventh chapter, I shed a little more clarity and coherence to the political debate between left and right. I will show how neither of the two options is morally superior to the other and what is the origin of the difference. I will show how the concepts of 'equality' and 'freedom' are the most relevant to understand an ideological stance. I will also question the accuracy of the division between left and right in a society as complex as ours.

In the same way, I will examine the duality of sex (man and woman) and gender (masculine and feminine) in the eighth chapter. Are they attributes that reduce and limit a much more complex reality? I will explain the reason behind the post-modern 'fluidity' in our gender roles, our sexuality and even our biology.

The opposition between reason and feelings is the engine driving the ninth chapter. It seems that we have shifted from an optimistic and rational era to a society that is fragmented into identity groups. Ideologically, many of these groups are driven by feelings and resentments; nevertheless, that doesn't make some of their demands invalid or worthless.

In a chapter dedicated to post-modern love, I will consider how the idea of love has changed over the centuries. I will talk about love in a pre-modern society and as it is considered today. I will also spend some time discussing the strange behaviour of the brain when it is in love.

The eleventh chapter deals with the issue of power from the perspective of our own bodies (bio-politics). I explain what this is, and how it appeared in some examples of our recent history. It is especially relevant in the case of those who oppose the use of vaccines and argue their right to decide.

I will end in the only way I can, by talking about death. It is not the intention here of giving a tragic vision of life or indulge in a morbid taste for lurid themes. I will simply show how 'death' is a slippery concept in post-modern philosophy that can mean different things. There is also an emphasis on how it is better not to avoid, or ignore, such an important topic which affects everyone (even if it is uncomfortable for most people).

I have included at the beginning of each chapter a brief introduction with some particular examples in order to capture your attention. They also help in better illustrating the topic in discussion and its connection with our daily life. And this is also an important point because none of the topics discussed in the book are merely speculative or treated at such a level of abstraction that they have no relation to us whatsoever. On the contrary, I believe that they all are issues of great importance for all of us owing to the implications they have for our present. One has to be very cold-blooded to feign disinterest on these topics.

The chapters do not need to be read in any particular order (and this, in itself, is already quite post-modern), although chapter one works as an introduction to all other chapters. You can decide if one topic interests you more than another. I, for my part, consider myself privileged if you read any of them.

CHAPTER 1

A NEW SOCIETY

*'Questioning the ostensibly unquestionable
premises of our way of life is arguably
the most urgent of services we owe
our fellow humans and ourselves'*

(Zygmunt Bauman)

Discussion

Can we argue that there is a new type of society with characteristics peculiar enough to distinguish it from modern society? What is post-modern society and what are its defining characteristics? How does that affect the lives of the individuals that comprise it? Are we immersed in a period of crisis like never before or rather do all values and customs enter into crisis periodically in history? Is there something that generates these crises?

Introduction

The spectacle was overwhelming. Groups of several hundred bloodied men stood in circles and whipped themselves on the back with a three-tailed whip to which sharp pieces of metal were attached.

Some women went out with rags to catch the drops of blood that spattered the walls and then rub their faces with them. They believed it had purifying qualities of highly spiritual power.

A master of ceremonies sang prayers, sometimes in Latin and sometimes in their vernacular language. The rest would repeat as if it were a litany. Meanwhile, they would continue whipping their naked bodies from the waist up. Once they finished, they fell to the ground and started all over again. The ritual was repeated three times, twice during the day and once during the afternoon. It was exhausting. It was purifying.

Although flogging was not a new ritual, in 1348 its public practice spread like wildfire. The penitents thought that God was punishing all mankind for their sins and all they wanted was to show repentance. They wanted to placate the wrath of God. However, the remedy did not seem to have an effect since the Black Death was rapidly decimating the population of almost all of Europe. It was the end of everything.

The flagellants traveled from town to town with the intention of not only saving themselves but also saving others. When they entered a new town the bells of the church announced their arrival. The neighbours came, completely open-mouthed to witness the bloody spectacle. If they mortified their bodies enough, as it happened to Jesus before dying on the cross, perhaps God would have mercy on them and end this plague that tormented everyone, especially the people of the cities.

Woodcut of flagellants (Nuremberg Chronicle, 1493).

The emergence of modernity

Mortality among the clergy was particularly high. The convents and nunneries were sources of contagion due to overcrowding in small spaces. These were favourable conditions for the rats that in turn carried the fleas transmitting the disease. This was, of course, not known until much later.[1]

Faced with this situation, the church saw the need to ordain more monks and nuns to compensate for the loss of its members. Many of the priests, understandably terrified, fled from the dying by refusing to give them last rites. At that time, dying without having received the Holy sacrament was

---

1. However, it is worth mentioning that scientist now believe that the plague spread too fast and humans, not rats, are the culprits.

the worst thing that could happen to a Christian person. The Church had to be creative in its solutions and to avoid greater evils the Pope blessed the waters of the Rhône river so that instead of burying the dead, they would be thrown into the waters and cleansed of any sin. It was also provided that if the dying could not find a priest, a 'normal man' was authorised to do so, and if none were willing, even a woman could do it. However, it was necessary for the Church to do a quick recruitment of new members, but this meant that many of the recruits joined without having any real vocation. They were motivated only for pure material interest and the consequences of that were soon felt. Corruption increased enormously and sometimes the sessions of public punishment ended in scenes of excessive alcoholism and sexual orgies.

The Renaissance author and Humanist, Giovanni Bocaccio describes in *The Decameron* the social collapse of the previous order in the following way:

Thus, doing exactly as they prescribed, they spend day and night moving from one tavern to the next, drinking without mode or measure, or doing the same thing in other people's homes, engaging only in those activities that gave them pleasure... And they combined this bestial behaviour with as complete avoidance of the ill as they could manage.

As a result of the Black Death, society changed a great deal. The feudal system and serfdom disappeared in much of Europe, especially in the North. It remained, however, in some areas such as the South of Italy. Over time this would lead to the development of the institution of the mafia, but that is another story. The peasants no longer depended on a feudal lord who owned all the land and who allowed them to use it in exchange for abusive percentages. It was a medieval and ineffective system of land exploitation since the peasants did not have enough motivation to increase crop production.

The flagellants (Pieter van Laer, 1635).

Interestingly, the material and economic conditions of the survivors improved substantially as well as the productivity of the land. After the enormous death toll caused by the Black Death epidemic, the workforce to plough the land and carry out other trades was scarce. Consequently, peasants and manual workers could demand a higher payment for their efforts and their products. In addition, a large part of capital and assets had been made available by the deaths of their former owners.

With the fear of the Black Death, religious sentiment increased, reaching its climax in the public martyrdom shows of the flagellants. However, with the evolution of the pandemic and the desolation it caused both in those who suffered from it and in the survivors, the attitude was changing. Some believed they saw God's disinterest in human affairs, but many others considered it a divine punishment for the corruption of the Church and its faithful. Consequently, society began to be more critical of the Church and its customs. In hindsight, it is easy to see how all this process had to culminate in something like the Protestant reform. Martin Luther rebelled against what he considered the moral decadence of the Catholic Church. The population, in response, was becoming somewhat secularised and paying more attention to 'human affairs' instead of the divine. This does not mean that the society completely lost faith, not least, since it remained deeply religious in many aspects. It happened, however, that people at the time started to relax their moral customs which in turn opened the way for a new line of thought: 'humanism'. It was a new way of thinking that put the human being, not God, at the centre of the universe. And that, in turn, laid the first solid stones of the Renaissance period.

The Dominican friar Girolamo Savonarola,
(Fra Bartolommeo di Pagholo, 1497).

It cannot be said that the Renaissance was a radical break with the past but rather a period of transformation that lasted several centuries. What the Renaissance did do was open the way for a new type of society that today we know as 'the Modern Age' or 'modernity'. During this time, the dominant values and ideas of the previous era were being replaced by new ones.

During the formation of Renaissance humanism, the education that was given in the universities of the time began to be questioned. That education was totally influenced by the church and scholasticism, both of which were gradually seen as obsolete and poorly adjusted to the new era. It was necessary to educate citizens in human matters, not purely in divine discussions. It was about training better speakers, lawyers, accountants, bankers, musicians, poets, etc. The model they were looking for was not that of the Middle Ages but that of classical Greek and Latin culture. They were searching for a balanced human being with an ideal of 'a healthy mind in a healthy body'. The world was changing and the seeds of the mercantile and capitalist system were being planted. Some city-states in Italy experienced a spectacular boom that made them the true centre of the Renaissance world. Venice, Milan and Florence were the epitome of refinement, luxury, art and power. But associated with the boom came corruption, debauchery, carnal pleasures - everything that had supposedly angered God and caused the Black Death. This time, however, someone had to stop it, and an Dominican monk thought he knew how to do it: Girolamo Maria Francesco Matteo, better known as Savonarola (1452-1498). He wanted to guide authentic Christians towards salvation. With his incendiary sermons in the city of Florence he earned the enmity of a large part of the ruling class, including the Pope of Rome and the

Medici family that had held the power in Florence for many decades.

His followers believed that he was a prophet and a visionary. Almost all of his predictions came true and he was preaching against luxury, the accumulation of wealth, inequality between rich and poor, art, sodomy, and vanity. His strong personality and his fanatical character led him to organise the most famous vanity bonfire in history. It took place in Florence on February 7, 1497 and in it he encouraged the Florentines to destroy in a purifying fire all objects considered sinful. These included prohibited books, works of art, clothes, makeup and in general any object considered luxurious, vain or superfluous.

Later, on 12 May Pope Alexander VI excommunicated Savonarola and threatened the Florentines with an interdict if they persisted in harbouring him. After describing the Church as a whore, Savonarola was excommunicated for heresy and sedition. Under torture Savonarola confessed to having invented his prophecies and visions, then recanted, then confessed again. On the morning of 23 May 1498, Savonarola and two monks were led out into the main square where, before a tribunal of high clerics and government officials, they were condemned as heretics and schismatics, and sentenced to die forthwith. Stripped of their Dominican garments in ritual degradation, they mounted the scaffold in their thin white shirts. Each on separate gallows, they were hanged, while fires were ignited below them to consume their bodies. To prevent devotees from searching for relics, their ashes were carted away and scattered in the Arno.

No one would be able to visit his grave. Although Savonarola's conservative revolution failed, it was the first strong reaction against the Renaissance mentality and clearly a precedent of the Lutheran reform of the Church.

As we can see, the changes introduced by the Renaissance did not happen overnight nor were they accepted by everyone. Authority figures such as Savonarola, Luther or Calvin were not happy with the new ideals of the Renaissance and believed that too much importance was attached to trade and the art of making money. On the contrary (they thought), the moral formation of the students, and the citizens in general, was being neglected.

The Renaissance opened the door to the later rationalism of the 16th and 17th centuries. This is an era marked by confidence in solving problems logically and mathematically. It is also at this time that science acquired a very important development. During the Enlightenment of the eighteenth century, intellectuals took the rationalist and scientific mentality of the preceding centuries to its ultimate consequences. A continuous search for 'the truth' began. Their intention was to correct the world with reason; or put differently, they were trying to create order in a chaotic nature. Enlightened thinkers aimed to reform, and to change an imperfect world. They strived to create a perfect one. To achieve this objective, they relied on reason, science and technology. However, this noble and seemingly unquestionably sensible goal had a fundamental problem: different people had different ideas about what a perfect world meant.

In history, there have been several attempts to create a perfect society, but in order to attain this ideal it has been necessary to make sacrifices, invade countries, exterminate populations, declare wars, etc. Some saw this as only a minor price for the accomplishment of the ultimate goal: paradise on earth.

As we will see in future chapters, in today's society there is great distrust of these major utopian projects at a global level. We have changed the 'social' goals for 'individual' ones as we increasingly live in a private sphere that we insist on making public (for example, through social media). In the West, universal visions of a perfect society are in decline. Instead, we are left with individual visions of a perfect life in a world that is far too heterogeneous to make any sense. In recent years, the literature about how to live the perfect life or attain happiness is enormous. Every author has a recipe.

The transition to post-modernity

Everything points to the fact that at the present time, we are in a process of transition similar to that of the Renaissance after the Black Death. The difference is that today we are experiencing a shift from modernity to post-modernity. However, all those changes in customs and values are (as it was the case in the Renaissance) neither immediate nor accepted by everyone. To help us understand these transitions, we can divide historical Western societies into three great moments: Pre-modern, modern and post-modern. Obviously, these are contemporary terms applied by historians and they were not used in the past.

The Pre-Modern society (the society before the Renaissance) has as its main characteristic a greater connection between all the phenomena of the universe. All knowledge was mixed as there was no clear distinction between causes and consequences. For example, a sudden death or a destructive storm were all connected with an astral conjunction of the planets. Likewise, a simple illness could be the consequence of cursing, or an evil eye. Everything was united and connected because everything had an ultimate cause with a very clear reason for being: 'God'. God was widely considered to be the centre of the entire universe. He was the one who ordered, punished, disposed of, rewarded, helped, inspired, etc. In pre-modern societies life had a simple and straightforward meaning. Each member of society had a well-defined role in the world and they knew exactly what to expect for the future.

As we have seen, the new world that is born after the Black Death and the Renaissance (the Modern Age) introduced a change, that was both gradual and discontinuous, by which the phenomena of the universe began to separate. It was a return to the old platonic idea of *symploke²*. In other words, the ideathat in this world not everything is connected with everything, but everything is connected with something else. As the sciences started to develop, they introduced a separation and established the points of union between different phenomena in the universe. For example, medicine showed that a fever is produced by biological causes other than astral conjunction. Consequently, the connection between body temperature and the position of the planets in the sky had been severed. Medicine and astronomy are two separate disciplines that are generally unrelated.

It is in this continuous separation from the previous unity that the need for God was gradually eliminated. In the pre-modern world, God intervened constantly, and was the glue that kept everything together. But as the modern period progressed, the role of God was increasingly reduced to an abstract presence that was limited to regulating the general functioning of the

---

2. *Symploke* is the idea that everything is connected to something else, excluding the possibility that everything is connected to everything. More graphically, it is like the knots in a fisherman's net.

universe. God began to look more like a mathematician or an architect who designed the general plan but did not intervene in every aspect of our lives. Or using a more recent metaphor, we could say that God went from micro-managing the world to delegating responsibility to human beings.

During the Modern Age, God was far from having disappeared, but his place was gradually being taken by the human being. Unlike God, humans are not omnipotent, but we can rationally explain a significant number of phenomena. In order to do that, we make use of reason and the causal explanation by which everything is the cause of something previous. Now, we do not really need God to explain most things because we just need to investigate and find the cause of any phenomenon.

The necessity of a God was not completely eliminated in the Modern Age. God was still necessary because otherwise rationality would have fallen into an infinite chain of causes and would never arrive at a principle. We could find the causes of a phenomenon without having to resort to God, true, but in the end we would need an ultimate cause that gives meaning to everything that exists. This is the so-called 'God of the philosophers', an abstract and metaphysical entity that has little to do with the personal God of Christianity, the one you can talk to. Isaac Newton (1642-1726) knew this very well. Thanks to his calculations and observations, he had been able to explain why the planets followed an orbit around the sun and did not collide with each other randomly. The laws of universal gravitation had made it clear that bodies with greater mass attracted the smaller ones and that is why the sun acted as a kind of magnet on the planets. However, Newton was aware that the laws of gravitation were only a partial answer to a much more general question. He expressed the need for a first cause when he said that gravity explained the motions of the planets, but could not explain who set them in motion. For Newton, as for everyone in the Modern Age, the answer was obvious, only God could perform that function.

As we will see in the following chapters of this book, the post-modern era in which we currently live is not a radical break with modernity since both overlap. As it also happened in the past, there must be a long period of transition between the two, and that period has not yet ended. In fact, it is not that this mentality will completely disappear (for example, there are people today who still believe that the alignment of the planets affects their lives directly). What does happen is that this type of mentality becomes less dominant or is systematically questioned.

Although it is debatable, there are many indications that the attitude that was prevalent during the Modern Age is today in crisis. In fact, post-modernity undoes the previous work of modernity. This means that post-modernity questions the barriers that divided knowledge. Medicine might not be connected with astrology, but medicine is not a neutral and objective knowledge either. There are many other factors that influence the medical practice: politics, religion, economy, society, etc. All of them are conditioning the type of medical knowledge that we get and the practices that are considered appropriate.

In this post-modern era there is no longer a unity of meaning and there cannot be a first cause as the origin (or engine) of all things. There are no Gods in post-modern society; only minor heroes are acceptable. Reality becomes multiple, the possible worlds are infinite. The barriers between the public and the private, between the personal and the political, between the real and the virtual, between the human and the animal, between the natural and the artificial, between the truth and the lie, etc. are all eliminated. We have reached a point where human beings are not the centre of the world either, in fact, there is no centre of the world. Our 'modern compass' does not work anymore.

Some post-modern philosophers even think that just as God had died, now it is the turn to bury the human subject. This might explain why some refer to our era as post-human-ism. In this context it is much more difficult to give a coherent meaning to life and there is constant talk of crisis: personal crisis, social crisis, cultural crisis, economic crisis, political cri-sis, moral crisis, etc. The institutions that previously regulated and gave order to our lives (Church, family, marriage, uni-versity, mass-media, political parties, trade unions, etc.) are losing power and authority. Many of these institutions are also competing with each other and this in turn generates more instability that ultimately translates into confusion, lack of direction, a feeling of being dazed, a crisis of vocation, de-pression, anxiety, etc. It is curious to note that although the current material conditions are much better today, the suicide rate in some Western countries is not necessarily lower[3].

There are also many (some would say 'too many') alternatives offered to counter this post-modern condition. Religions, for instance, continue to offer an alternative of unity of life and a long-term vital project with very clear rules and limits. Religion continues to be very attractive for many people today, especially in times of confusion. Others prefer to turn to spiritual advi-

---

3. According to the House of Commons Library In 2021 there were 6,319 deaths registered in Great Britain where the cause was recorded as suicide.
   Relative to the size of the population, the suicide rate in England and Wales has declined by 28% since 1981. However, most of this fall occurred before 2000. In 2021 the rate was higher than it had been in 2005-2012 and 2016-2017.

sors, life-coaches, astrologers, influencers, charity work, gurus, self-help programs, psychological therapies, diets and so on.

In a post-modern society, changes are fast and constant. There is not enough time for the new to solidify and become institutionalised into firm structures that can last for several generations. The only thing that remains unchanged is the need for change itself. Post-modern societies do not cling to anything from the past and do not look to the future either. The post-modern is, notoriously, a society of the present. The important thing is the 'here and now' and tomorrow will be a different 'here and now'. Our ideas about education, sex, politics, aesthetics, food, etc. are in a permanent flow and we do not know where they come from or where they are going.

Unlike what happened in modernity, today there is a greater emphasis on individual progress, and not enough on social progress. We are more about personal improvement, empowerment courses, entrepreneurism, applications to increase productivity and exercise to improve health and looks. There is a focus on achieving partial goals that are supposed to improve our lives as a whole. To make matters worse, the competition is constant and everywhere. If we do not improve ourselves, others will do it, and it will be painful to see how others achieve their goals and we don't. We are scared that our neighbour will live the fuller life we aspire to. Nobody wants to be a 'loser'.

Byun-Chul Han (1959) is a strange case in contemporary philosophy. Born in South Korea, he began university studies in metallurgy, but he did not find the motivation to complete them. He actually wanted to study literature, but that wouldn't be possible in Korea since his family would never allow it. To make his wish a reality, he moved to Germany, but there was an added problem, he didn't speak a word of German. This would always be a handicap in a degree where students had to read many books in a short period of time. Finally, he had to change Literature for Philosophy where, according to his own account, he could read more slowly. He got his PhD in 1994 and, little by little, began to publish short books that are now best sellers in the field of Philosophy.

According to Byun-Chul Han we have internalised the idea of being constantly productive. He believes that during the Modern Age some individuals exploited others. Factory employees working long hours for low wages would be a good example of this. In today's post-modern society, although something from the previous era still persists, the exploiters are in decline because we exploit ourselves. It is a much more subtle and less violent exploitation than the previous one and, of course, less likely to provoke riots. Individuals who exploit themselves are more docile and less aggressive. They do not have time to revolt, they are too busy being busy. In contrast to what happened in the past, our post-modern society is not a disciplinary one in which there is a superior authority (political, religious, racial, tribal, etc.) that dominates us. In Western democracies there are no more masters and slaves because we now live in a society obsessed with performance and productivity. Freedom, paradoxically, has made us free from others but slaves to ourselves. According to Han, today's mental problems no longer arise due to the repression of others, but rather are problems of the self: depression, hyperactivity, burnout, attention problems, etc.

The structure of our economic production has also changed. The differences between agricultural workers, industrial workers and white-collar professions have vanished. They all are a form of business, they all produce something that has to be sold. Even farmers buy in supermarkets what they produce. It is rather an economy of consumption and not so much of production.

The same thing would happen with some of our experiences. They become objects of consumption and symbols of status. A trip to Paris becomes an object of consumption when we share all the photos on social media doing all the things we are supposed to do or eating what the trend of the moment tells us to. In post-modern societies the image is more important than the content or the ideology. Some political parties are aware of this power and pay young and attractive influencers to spread their message and attract new voters.

Besides, in a post-modern society the amount of information available is so big and so varied that it becomes irrelevant. We constantly see how information is being transformed into entertainment as the only way to make it relevant for people. Education in post-modern societies is frequently linked to the idea of 'learning by playing' or at least, having fun while learning. The gamification of academic content is one of the priorities of many educational institutions. This is not necessarily a bad thing because some studies demonstrate the effectiveness of the game as an educational strategy. The problem, however, is the trivialisation of some content, or the idea that 'traditional study' is bad.

Another very interesting feature of post-modern society is the reduction of intimate space. Emotional nudity (real or fictitious) is not seen as a weakness, quite the opposite. The smallest details of a relationship or everyday life are shared on social media. Some of the most popular programs on television publicly detail the intimate life of relationships, a family or work colleagues. The public sphere is confused with the private one. Nothing really shocks anymore; it just goes viral for a short period of time and then disappears. Yesterday's taboos have become objects of consumption: T-shirts promoting drugs, offensive tattoos, memes with porn actors, etc.

Some young Japanese lock themselves in their room to avoid the pressures of the outside world.

Traditions are losing their importance in post-modern societies. Individuals have greater decision-making power and do not have to follow in their parents' footsteps. They decide what religion they ascribe to, what they want to study, what industry they prefer to work in, the place they want to live or the person with whom to start a family. This, in turn, entails the need to be constantly choosing. We are continuously 'forced' to select one option from the many possible alternatives, knowing that we can make a mistake in our choice and regret it later. As existentialist French thinkers pointed out, to live in our society means to choose, and choosing generates anxiety and uncertainty. Our jobs, partners, cars, houses, etc. they all are the result of our choices, and (although in reality they are not), in post-modern society it is seen that way. We assume that we decide our fate, that we are masters of our own destiny. If we don't get what we want is because we don't try hard enough. There is no one else to blame and the responsibility lies with us. This type of mentality can cause anguish in some people and make psychological therapies a necessity in our society, even among the youngest.

A particular case of this situation is the *hikikomori* of Japan. These are young people who renounce all social contact and live secluded in their rooms, although they do it in their parents' house. In the most extreme cases, they do not leave their rooms even to eat and only go to the bathroom when they are sure that nobody will see them. They can spend many years in this situation, and sometimes even decades. Although it is a typically Japanese problem, there are more and more cases in other countries. These are usually middle and upper-middle class males who develop acute symptoms of agoraphobia and social anxiety.

It is difficult to give an exact figure for the number of *hikikomori* in Japan because their parents often do not seek help or admit that there is a problem. They are simply too ashamed that their children are confined to their rooms and refuse to work or study. In any case, some estimates tell us of nearly a million *hikikomoris* in Japan alone.

Although there are different causes, psychologists have detected that young Japanese males, in particular, feel overwhelmed by the demands of the society in which they live and the pressure to fulfil a certain social role. They want to stay away from the responsibilities and constant decisions making that adult life entails. In addition, the pressure to achieve good academic results is enormous. Competition among young people is fierce in the highly selective Japanese job market. Faced with the demands of their families and society in general, their response is to withdraw in their rooms and communicate with the outside world only through electronic devices and the Internet. Some refer to them as the post-modern hermits.

Conclusion

Even if we accept that we live in a time of crisis, it cannot be said that it is something exclusive to our age. Throughout history, times of crisis can be easily traced. Examples include the fall of the Roman Empire, society after the Black Death, or the European existentialism after World War II.

Bertrand Russell, describing the situation in the fifteenth century, noted the following:

Emancipation from the church led to the growth of individualism, even to the point of anarchy. Discipline, intellectual, moral, and political, was associated in the minds of men of the Renaissance with the scholastic government. The Aristotelean logic of schoolmen was narrow, but afforded a training in a certain kind of accuracy. When this school of logic became unfashionable, it was not at first, succeeded by something better, but only by an eclectic imitation of ancient models. Until the 17th century, there was nothing of importance in Philosophy. The moral and political anarchy of 15th century Italy was appalling (...) at the same time, the freedom from mental shackles led to an astonishing display of genius in art and literature. But such society is unstable.

Modernity wanted the members of society to emancipate themselves from oppressive and ineffective institutions and values. They used reason and science as a weapon to fight against them and free society from that tyrannical power. However, post-modernity sees a contradiction in this since the well-intentioned and rational project of modernity generated another equally repressive system in which there was no place for what was out of the norm: religious or ethnic minorities, homosexuals, left-handed people, alternative medicine, the mythology of

other cultures, etc. This is the reason why in post-modern societies there is an emphasis on giving visibility and 'normalizing'
these minorities and alternative views. Post-modern thinkers
are committed to present possible options to the knowledge
that modernity considered objective, natural or immutable.
The aim of post-modern philosophy is to eradicate the 'oppres-
sion' from definitive answers (truths), rational thinking (logic)
and the hierarchy of knowledge (sciences).

Schematically we can see the differences between both societies in the following table:

MODERN SOCIETY	POST-MODERN SOCIETY
Stable social structures: families, gender roles, class, etc.	Less stable structures: fluidity, social mobility, etc.
Institutions like churches, schools, political parties, companies, etc. are relevant in people's life.	Institutions are less relevant in our life and they lose their authority.
Permanent relationships that last a lifetime.	Less meaningful and transient relationships with friends, family, partners, colleagues, etc.
Long-term planning.	Short-term thinking.
Past is a good indicator of how the future will be.	Past is not a reliable source of information for future planning.
Choices are limited.	More choice equals more responsibility.
Long-term strategies.	Opportunism.
Socially oriented.	Individually oriented.
Belief in unquestionable truths.	Truth equals totalitarianism, impositions and violence.
Individuals rooted in tradition and certainty.	Fear of uncertainty.

CHAPTER 2

TRUTH AND POST-TRUTH

*'There are no facts,
only interpretations.'*

(Nietzsche)

Discussion

In our Western societies we question the veracity of almost any-thing, but that was not the case in the past. What has changed? Is truth something objective or can we argue that it is subjective? Can we talk about only one type of truth or are there others? What is the connection between truth and power? Is the word 'narrative' the substitute for 'truth'? Is lying necessarily the opposite of 'truth'? Does the truth change over time or is it immutable?

Introduction

When Monica finished her studies in psychology in 1995, she had a bright future ahead of her. However, by July of that same year, she started a work placement at the White House that would change her life forever.

Little could she imagine that at only 22 years old, she would become the most wanted person by the press, not only in her country but all over the world. Her last name, 'Lewinsky', would become synonymous with scandal, and she would be the subject of countless jokes and derogatory comments. Nothing would ever be the same for her, and neither would it be for the then President of the United States of America.

The case is very well known. Between 1995 and 1997, William Jefferson Clinton and Monica Lewinsky had a minimum of nine sexual encounters which, if they came to light, would put the President's political career at risk. The President's team knew first-hand what was happening and was fully aware of the possible consequences. The relationship became so dangerous that Clinton's advisers decided to remove Monica Lewinsky from the Oval Office before the scandal broke. As their sexual games were getting more and more careless, she was offered a different role at the Pentagon.

The affair would have remained secret if it were not for Monica's friend, Linda Tripp. In private telephone conversations, Lewinski began to give juicy details about her numerous encounters with the President. Tripp was 22 years older than Monica and knew that she was onto something big. She secretly recorded those conversations for 'patriotic reasons', as she later stated. The moment the recordings became public, one of the biggest scandals in American politics broke out.

Bill Clinton and Monica Lewinski in February 1997.

Both the President and Lewinsky tried to deny the case, but their credibility was seriously compromised. Monica, as it was later revealed, had been in a secret relationship for several years with another married man. The person in question was her high school drama teacher while she was still his student. The affair was over after she graduated, but it wasn't doing her public image any favours. In Clinton's case, his extramarital affairs were well known, particularly after the Paula Jones case, in which Clinton was indicted in 1994 for sexual harassment. Previously, there was the Gennifer Flowers affair: a civil servant who in 1992 declared that she had had a 12-year relationship with Clinton, the then-candidate for the White House.

Many Americans were shocked by the behaviour of their president. They criticised the fact that he cheated on his wife. If he was capable of doing that, what would he be capable of as President of the United States? His moral values were clearly not in tune with the public persona that he portrayed.

Clinton vehemently denied having a sexual relationship with Monica Lewinsky, but incriminating evidence appeared. More specifically, a blue cocktail dress containing semen stains. The sample was analysed and the results unequivocally proved that the President had lied to the whole nation while under oath.

The consequences of perjury (lying when you have an obligation to tell the truth) could be disastrous for the President. In fact, it was the beginning of an 'impeachment' process in which he could be removed from post. However, Clinton's defence strategy surprised everyone as they had an ace in the hole.

At a solemn moment in his statement, he asked to read a note that he thought would clarify the whole situation. From the left pocket of his jacket, he took out a piece of paper that he carefully unfolded. He put on his reading glasses and in a serious voice acknowledged that his behaviour had not been appropriate:

'When I was alone with Miss Lewinsky on certain occasions in 1996, and once in 1997, I engaged in contact that was wrong.'

It was the first admission that they had had physical contact, but he did not specify the type of contact they had. The President also claimed that he had not lied in his previous statement. Although without any specifics, his reasoning was that since it was only oral sex that Lewinsky performed on him, and there was no penetration, then it could not be regarded as a sexual relationship. His role had been passive. He did not lie.

'These encounters did not consist of sexual intercourse. They did not constitute sexual relationships as I understood that term to be defined.... but it did involve inappropriate intimate contact.'

He considered that he was not active in these encounters, and consequently it could not be called a proper sexual relationship. Furthermore, when he was asked about the veracity of having a sexual relationship with Ms Lewinsky, the investigator used the present tense 'is', instead of the past tense 'was'. Clinton famously retorted:

'It depends on what the meaning of the word 'is' is.'

He denied having a relationship with her at the present time (*'there is no'*), but he did not necessarily deny that there was some kind of sexual relationship in the past. He never said that *'There* was *not a sexual relationship with Monica Lewinsky'*. That would have been lying, but in fact he was truthful. His voters, though, were less interested in such linguistic technicalities.

Different meanings of 'truth'

The story of Bill Clinton and Monica Lewinsky is well documented and is a reminder of how elusive is the concept of 'truth' and how many different interpretations it can have. For instance, if we try to find what the opposite of 'truth' is, we are presented with several possibilities: 'lie', 'error', 'deception', 'concealment', 'falsehood', 'perjury', etc. Clinton was probably responsible for all of them, but each one has its own particular connotation.

As the President's lawyers knew very well, we will have different meanings depending on the context in which we use the word 'truth'. To prove this point, it will be necessary to show how the term can be used in a variety of contexts, each one with a specific meaning. The problem emerges when these different meanings get mixed up in an argument about 'the truth of something', as it creates a lot of confusion.

Let's consider four different scenarios:

1. Truth as a revelation. In a religious context, the truth is something revealed by some divine entity. We cannot reach this truth by any method other than through faith. Religions have a very rigid idea of truth as it is something that cannot be doubted. Rational discussion is neither necessary nor enough to justify (or attack) a religious truth. In John 14:6, Jesus says, *'I am the way, and the truth, and the life.'* A Christian will believe this. However, a Muslim will not. In the Islamic world, there is a different 'truth'. There is no possible agreement between Christians and Muslims and in the end, it is a matter of faith. Besides, even within the same religion, the truth can be a matter of interpretation. Divisions, schisms, theological disputes and reforms are common in any main religion. Christians are divided between Catholics, Lutherans, Calvinists, Orthodox, Seventh-day Adventists, Jehovah's Witnesses, Evangelists, Anabaptists and many others. In Islam, there are Sunnis, Shiites, Wahhabis, Muslim brothers, Alawites, etc. All of them are clearly competing for one 'Truth'. Initially, Bill Clinton asked Americans to believe him with no other proof than faith in his words as President.

2. Truth and science. In science, there is an attempt to define 'truth' in a more precise and objective sense. In this case, scientific truths are independent of the faiths, desires, beliefs

and the will of any individual. When we speak of 'truth' in science, we can distinguish two types:

A- Logical (or formal) truths. In this case, the validity of the truth is given by its formal structure. For example: 'A triangle has three sides'. To deny the validity of this would be absurd as the definition is implicit in its name. Clinton's linguistic tricks would go in this direction. He wanted to prove that no lie can be deduced from the literal interpretation of his words, he was honest in responding with logical truths.

B- Material (or empirical) truths. It is necessary to refer to experience to confirm the truth of what is stated. For example: 'If we heat water to 100 degrees Celsius, it starts to boil'. We need to do different experiments to confirm the truth of the statement before we declare it true. To deny the validity of this statement is not a logical inconsistency as it could be that under certain circumstances (altitude for instance) the boiling point is at a lower temperature. The prosecutor in the Clinton case tried to show the truth of his theory, that is to say that there were sexual relations between the President and Monica Lewinski, based on a scientific truth (the DNA test of the dress).

3. In legal contexts we use a somewhat different definition of truth. It is as if we were trying to place a mirror to a reality that is considered objective. Telling the truth in a legal case would consist of turning our words into a reflection of 'reality'. However, to do the opposite would not necessarily be lying, since a witness can make mistakes. People can involuntarily deceive themselves or they can draw a wrong conclusion. Bill Clinton drew a very different conclusion from the

prosecutor when he said that oral sex did not count as a sexual relationship. They might be referring to the same situation but the words used to describe it (the mirror) have a filter that carries different connotations. The reality that Clinton tried to show with his words is that in their meetings there was no sexual relationship if we base ourselves on the facts (there was no penetration).

4. Pragmatic truth. This is a more practical approach. 'Truth' is understood as something that works well, or at least something that produces positive results. If something is useful and works well, then it is true. For example, in the medical field, if something remedies the problem, then it is 'true'. It is validated by its effectiveness in solving a problem. For Clinton's team of advisers, the truth about the affair is that it would not be a problem anymore if Monica was moved to a different building (as she was). It worked perfectly.

Is there really 'the truth'?

We could continue considering different contexts, and the term 'truth' will keep having different meanings. We could question ourselves, for example, if there is 'the truth' in History, in Ethics or in Politics. Are we perhaps using the appropriate terms or words? Is there really 'a truth' to what happened in the battle of Hastings? We can agree in the fact that there was a fight in the year 1066 between the Anglo-Saxons and the Normans. We could even say that it is true that there was such a thing as a battle in a place called Hastings but not so much about the real causes and consequences or the exact number of people involved.

On a different context, can we even accept that there are ethical truths (also known as 'Natural Law') such as "all individuals have a right to life"? And if so, does it also apply to an embryo in a mother's womb? In other words, is there a truth in the debate about abortion? Or, can 'the truth' of the Lewinsky affair ever be established? Is it true that there was a sexual relationship? And even if we accept that truth really does exist in these contexts, what kind of truth are we talking about? Is it logical, revealed, formal, pragmatic or is it some kind of social consensus that we later label with the name 'truth'?

There is no doubt that the question is complicated, but it is also an important one. At first glance, it would seem that there are some truths that are truer than others, which is in itself a contradiction. If we add 2+2, the result will always be 4, and the veracity of this truth cannot be doubted, or... maybe it could?

The French philosopher René Descartes (1596–1650) was concerned with these questions. His mother died shortly after giving birth and when he was just 10 years old his father, who was a councillor in the Parliament of Brittany, sent him to the most prestigious boarding school in France where he received an elite education. There he was for 8 years and in the final courses he devoted himself fully to the study of logic, philosophy and mathematics. He was aware that he had received the best education that could be obtained at that time, but he also knew that the knowledge he had acquired was not supported by a solid foundation, perhaps with the exception of mathematics. He realised that in reality he could not be sure about anything he was taught. Descartes thought that he was lacking a durable truth in his knowledge that would guarantee the validity of anything else.

Although it may seem strange to us now, after graduating from the university of Poitiers he dedicated himself to serving in different armies as a soldier at the same time that he published treatises on mathematics. In November 1619, after a few years of travelling and military service, he had three consecutive dreams in which he clearly saw what his life goal was: to find 'the truth' with the simple use of reason. He wanted to establish a new discipline, a 'wonderful science' as he described it, that would underpin all knowledge. He set himself the task of finding a truth so obvious and so evident that it would be impossible not to accept it. He was looking for 'the biggest truth' of them all. Mathematical truths ($2 + 2 = 4$) seemed like a good candidate, but Descartes did not want to accept it as indubitable either. What if there were (at least hypothetically) an evil God that makes us wrong every time we add 2+2. We could be deceived, unknowably, by this evil God and think that the correct result is four, when in reality, it is something different.

For Descartes, doubting was the absolute truth that could not be doubted. Doubting is an indication that we think and thinking is the proof that we exist. Hence, the famous phrase that is frequently repeated when talking about Descartes: *I think; therefore I am.* However, a more accurate description would be: 'I doubt; therefore I think. I think; therefore I am'.

The interesting thing about Descartes's rhetorical argument is that we can even doubt maths, science or anything that seems to be absolutely true. This way of thinking was labelled 'methodical doubt' and is a radical disbelief in the truth of anything. However, this distrust in the truths of our knowledge is only of a theoretical nature as it does not affect the belief in the truths of everyday life such as 'if it rains I get wet' or 'if I put my hand near the fire I will get burnt'. However, there was nothing that really supported the truth of these things, and Descartes himself had to resort to the existence of God (this time, it had to be a good one) to guarantee the truth of everything else.

Critics of Descartes say that first he frees himself from the need for God and then reintroduces the idea of God into his system as a guarantee for the world to make sense. In this case, he reminds us of Newton a few years later when he needed God to set the planets in motion, which later moved independently around the Earth.

Thanks to the security offered by having God as the basis of knowledge and the universe, the truths during the Modern Age acquire an eternal dimension. However, today we know that 'truth' can also be fleeting. Many of the theories that were considered to be true in the time of Descartes were later proven false. Hence, the truth can also be something temporary. Our assumptions of today will be proven false or unfounded in the future. The truths of today will be the 'lies' of tomorrow. This is a fundamental change in our post-modern society. What we consider to be true, or good, or fair or impossible to change is not necessarily the case anymore. For Descartes or Newton, marriage would only be conceivable between a man and a woman. Being vegan would never be seen as better than a diet that included meat. To question the existence of God would be a logical contradiction... but as we see, all these 'truths' are openly questioned in our current society.

Post-truth and narratives

The use of the term 'narrative' in the media has become widespread in recent years. In many instances, it is used as an alternative to the word 'truth'. One of the main reasons ford this change is because 'truth' has the connotation of being too arrogant and exclusive. 'The truth' is not a 'democratic' idea because it leaves out many alternative narratives that also claim to be true.

This idea of 'narrative' fits much better in today's society. The door is left open to other stories or narratives. It is a more inclusive term than 'truth'. Speaking in the name of truth can be seen as authoritarian, and it is perceived as leading to a totalitarian way of thinking.

Scientists, however, are appalled when people with no academic background start questioning what they consider to be unquestionable. For instance, in some schools in the United States, the evolution theory is explained as one narrative. At the same time, the idea that the world was created by God in seven days is also explained as an alternative narrative. At this point, the truth is fragmented and gives raise to the idea of 'post-truth'.

To be more precise, we can point to the year 2016 as a key moment in the spread of the term 'post-truth'. Two political events which had great international repercussions occurred that year: the election of Donald Trump as President of the United States and the referendum on the permanence of the United Kingdom in the European Union (Brexit).

In this historical context, the Oxford English language dictionary chose the term 'post-truth' as the most important word of the year. The supporters of conflicting political ideas were constantly accusing each other of manipulating information and using fallacious reasoning. They disqualified the arguments of their rivals as 'post-truth'.

However, 2016 was not the year when the term 'post-truth' was born, as it was Steve Tesich (1942-1996) who introduced it in 1992. Best known for being the winner of an Oscar for the screenplay *'Breaking Away'* (1979), Steve Tesich came to the United States from the former Yugoslavia when he was 14 years old. He graduated from college and had some success as a writer of plays and novels. Unfortunately, he died prematurely at age 53 from a heart attack. In an essay from 1992 entitled *A Government of Lies,* Tesich denounced that the population of the United States had come to associate 'truth' with something uncomfortable, a kind of nuisance that was difficult to accept. People seem to prefer the state to protect them from the truth. It is this attitude of self-denial that allows us to start talking about post-truth because it is preferable that the mirror does not reflect reality 'as it is'. The general public does not want to know the darkest aspects of the truth. At that time, the 'truths' Tesich was referring to were the economic crisis, the political scandals, the Gulf War, the information on the Watergate case, the reports on the tortures of the Vietnam War, etc. It is better to build an alternative reality, kinder and more suited to our interests. Post-truth is a distorted image produced by a mirror that only reflects what we want to see and hides what we do not want to show. Tesich puts it this way:

'All the dictators up to now have had to work hard at suppressing the truth. We, by our actions, are saying that this is no longer necessary, that we have acquired a spiritual mechanism that can denude truth of any significance. In a very fundamental way, we, as a free people, have freely decided that we want to live in some post-truth world.'

This is the first documented use of the term 'post-truth'. However, the idea is not new at all, nor was Tesich the first to make a similar criticism. Tesich took up the idea from the

German philosopher Friedrich Nietzsche (1844–1900). In a text entitled *On Truth and Lies in a Nonmoral Sense*, Nietzsche wrote the following:

> *'Man only desires the truth in an analogous and limited sense: he longs for the pleasant consequences of the truth, those that sustain life; it is indifferent to pure knowledge without consequences, and he is even hostile to truths susceptible to damaging or destructive effects.'*

Today, the concept of post-truth is fully accepted and is used to describe a situation in which there is manipulation, propaganda, deception, fraud, etc. It is closely linked with another new term, 'post-factual'. Now it is relatively common to cherry-pick data and reach any conclusion we like. With the technological development that we have, it is possible to access more information and data than ever before. Contrary to popular belief, public access to this information has not led to greater clarity in discussions. On the contrary, it has produced a deeper division in which each side feels justified by the force of facts and numbers. The same data constantly produces different conclusions.

Nietzsche and Tesich understood the idea of 'post-truth' as self-deception or not wanting to see a harsh and difficult reality. Today, the term is understood as an ideological manipulation, a distortion of facts with the aim of challenging the veracity of political and ideological rivals. The best way to achieve this goal is by appealing directly to emotions and not wasting time with rational arguments, data or facts that contradict our preconceived ideas.

It is this very idea that we can still talk about 'objective facts' that have been under question in recent years. It became particularly obvious in political debate, but also in social media and journalism in general. Reality, as we came to know it, is just one of the many possible narratives. The truth is only the most suitable version for the ruling powers. Truth is relative, not absolute, and in today's society, it lacks the force that it once had. It is an increasingly common tendency among some student bodies to prevent speakers from talking about subjects which those students find inconvenient, unpalatable or offensive. 'Alternative facts' are presented with the intention of dismantling rival accounts or simply to support the most convenient version. It is also common among the general public of today to have a skeptical attitude with regards to 'official truths'. These "imposed truths" are considered to be only lies, or in the best of cases half-truths. Conspiracy theories pop up everywhere and they are proposed as alternatives seeking to destabilise the establishment or the opinion of the adversaries.

Post-truth in the media

In recent years, journalism has changed enormously. The sources of information are so many and so contradictory that it is difficult to distinguish the wheat from the chaff. Until the 1990s, 24-hour information channels did not exist, but today they are the norm. The need to generate new information to fill hours of content is enormous. This means that the sources might not always be verified. In addition, with the appearance of free digital newspapers, the traditional printed ones have had to cut expenses. One journalist has to cover a greater number of assignments, and sometimes the quality of the reporting suffers.

The lack of informative rigour, together with the noise of social media, help the spread of false rumours. Some channels and media outlets feed the confusion instead of clarifying it. It is also very noticeable the ideological drift of some traditional media that now use personal disqualification as a way to refute arguments. One of the most common strategies of today is the use of *'ad hominem'* argumentation. This is a very old resource that consists of disqualifying an argument not because of its content but because of the person who transmits it. For example, if a very unpopular politician states that it is necessary to reform the pension system to ensure its soundness, the argument will be invalidated regardless of the data provided. If the person is very unpopular, therefore the argument must be wrong.

It is not a secret that the same facts and figures can have a different interpretation in the competing media channels. For instance, when a government official announces a decrease in the rate of economic growth, those in favour of the Government tend to see it as fair and adjusted to the situation. In contrast, those who are against the party in power tend to see it as insufficient and a proof of the incompetence of the government.

In this climate of constant mistrust, social media platforms play a central role in the creation of the ever-present 'fake news'. Why is this news so popular? Why don't we just ignore it? Neurology and cognitive linguistics deal with these questions and they offer us a rather convincing answer: this type of news has a greater impact on people if the information is conveyed in simple metaphors (or narratives) that appeal to emotion. This type of news has a greater social value, and they are more likely to be shared than those that are simply based on data and rational arguments. Usually, the most shared news has an emotional component attached to it.

Until not too long ago, the censorship of certain works and ideas generated a lot of interest for the simple fact of being prohibited. What could be more exciting than the books that religious leaders considered sinful? What philosophers could be more interesting than those considered to be 'dangerous'? This type of censorship, although effective in the short term, was almost never effective in the medium or long term. Where there is a desire, individuals will find a way to satisfy it. Curiosity about forbidden things is not something new and it has a long tradition in our society. In the Bible, just think of Eve being tempted with apples from the forbidden tree.

Currently, it would not be popular to impose such censorship but there are mechanisms (conscious or unconscious) that are more subtle and effective. They work by killing our curiosity, 'bombarding' everyone with a constant flow of new, and ever-changing information (often contradictory) that overwhelms individuals in such a way that nothing is relevant anymore. It is difficult to track down an article that is more than two days old in a digital newspaper. Furthermore, any opinion or idea can be countered by an extraordinary number of opinions in the opposite direction (whether they are well argued or not). We could explain it more graphically by saying that there are two ways of blinding a person: one is total darkness; but the other consists of dazzling a spotlight directly into the eyes. The first is common in modern society; the second in post-modern.

The result is total confusion, a lack of reference due to overabundance of information. There is also the feeling that everything is in a constant state of change, making it almost impossible to pass judgment on any subject. Lyrically, the Italian singer Franco Battiato (1945-2021) defined this uneasy feeling of crisis in post-modern societies in one of his songs:

I am looking for a permanent centre of gravity that does not change what I now think of things and people.

Origins of the change

Societies are constantly evolving, but where can we find the intellectual roots of the changes that we are talking about? Where do we look for an intellectual origin for this shift in the modern paradigm? Can we trace the evolution of thought and find clues to understand this transformation? The 'mental maps' we used to navigate through society just a few years ago are now obsolete. We need new ones, but also, we need to understand why.

Indeed, it is possible to trace a line of thought that explains how we arrived at the present situation, but in order to do this, it will be necessary to go further back in time. We will need to refer again to the transition from modernity to post-modernity.

As we have seen in the previous chapter, after the Middle Ages, during the Renaissance of the fifteenth and sixteenth centuries, a very important change began to take place, especially when we compare it to the previous era. Together with technological developments, a new greater interest in scientific and rational explanations began. In fact, a new type of philosophical thinking called 'rationalism' started to develop. It was the consolidation of a revolutionary idea: that everything could be explained rationally, and therefore it was possible to find absolute truths, particularly in the sciences, that were previously only found in religion or in a completely separate world (as Plato described when he mentioned the differences between this material world and the world of pure ideas)[4].

Science and religion began to clash because they both offered a really 'strong' idea of truth that at times came into contradiction. As it is perfectly documented, the Italian astronomer Galileo Galilei had to present himself in Rome before an inquisitorial court.

Galileo drank directly from the ideas of Copernicus who thought that the sun (not the Earth) was at the centre of the universe and that we revolved around it. Copernicus at the time was considered by many the laughingstock of Europe, a complete pariah. With a theory so ridiculous and contrary to experience, he clearly couldn't tell himself that he cared about the truth. 'The truth' is what appeared in the Bible and that was not debatable.

Thanks to the measurements and observations that Galileo was able to make when he invented the telescope, he confirmed Copernicus's theories, but almost no one was willing to accept it. Galileo thought that the Bible was indeed the word of God, but it was not a good astronomy book. In his opinion, mathematics was the language of God. Mathematics was exact and his calculations showed that the earth rotates on its axis and at the same time around the sun.

Galileo was accused of heresy and he had to publicly retract the idea that the Earth revolved around the sun and not vice

---

4. Near the end of the *Phaedo*, Plato describes the world of Forms as a pristine region of the physical universe located above the surface of the Earth (*Phd.* 109a–111c). In the *Phaedrus* the Forms are in a "place beyond heaven" *(huperouranios topos)* (*Phdr.* 247c ff).

versa. During the process, one of the doctors of the Church considered his theory to be:

'...silly and philosophically absurd, and formally heretical, since it explicitly contradicts in many places the meaning of Holy Scripture.'

Galileo in turn considered that scientific truth coincided with the truth of God but not necessarily with the truth of the Church. It may be an apocryphal quote (or an old example of 'fake news'), but it seems that when he publicly retracted his theory, he quietly said, *'Eppure si muove'* (And yet it moves)[5]. Galileo was not sentenced to burn at the stake like others did, but he had to remain under house arrest for the rest of his life. He died eight years later.

During the Modern Age, scientific advances were enormous in fields like astronomy (Copernicus, Kepler, Galileo), mathematics (Descartes, Leibniz) and physics (especially Newton).

As we will see in more detail later on, the Enlightenment of the eighteenth century reached the peak of modernity. The philosophers of that time almost completely dispensed with religious explanations, replacing them with other rational and scientific arguments. It does not mean that they stopped be-

---

5. According to available evidence, Galileo Galilei never said these notoriously famous words. They are not mentioned in judiciary files from the trial, neither in Galileo's own letters and other writings.

First recorded mention of this famous quote being said by Galileo comes from more than 120 years later, from notoriously inaccurate work "The Italian Library", written by Giuseppe Baretti. However, there is a very high probability that he either imagined this event himself, or took it from other dubious sources. "The moment Galileo was set free, he looked up to the sky and down to the ground, and, while stamping his foot, in a contemplative mood, he said, Eppur si muove, that is, and yet it moves, meaning the planet earth."

lieving or that they were atheists, but at least God was not the explanation for everything. They believed that 'the truth' was being discovered little by little, but inexorably. However, some post-modern critics say that they were just substituting one grand narrative for another narrative equally grand. Traditional religion was being substituted by a new religion: Science.

The image of 'nature' during the Romanticism (David Friedrich, 1818).

With the emergence of Romanticism at the end of the eighteenth century, cracks began to appear in the optimism of modernity. Confidence in reason and science was being lost. It was thought that reason alone would not set people free; something else was needed. Romantic thinkers believed that there was one part of human beings that was not rational, and authors like Friedrich Nietzsche wanted to make that point very clear. According to the German philosopher, the Western tradition (since Socrates in the fifth century BC until his day) had forgotten the irrational side of humans and had focused on the purely rational side of life. For Nietzsche, Christianity was the great enemy because it forgot the flesh and dealt only with the soul. The balance between rational and irrational that Nietzsche believed existed in ancient Greece (before Socrates) had been lost. Humans were not only rational beings; there was something in them that could not be explained with rational arguments[6].

Sigmund Freud (1856–1939) came to a similar conclusion, although he believed he was working in science, not philosophy. He noticed that the non-rational part of human beings was largely unconscious, and it tended to be repressed by the rational part and the rules of society. This imbalance generated an inner tension that leads to neurosis and other mental illnesses that, until that moment, were not taken into consideration and sometimes they did not even have a name.

---

6. The Apollonian and the Dionysian are philosophical and literary concepts represented by a duality between the figures of Apollo and Dionysus from Greek mythology.

   The concepts were made popular by the work *The Birth of Tragedy* by Friedrich Nietzsche, though the terms had already been in use prior to this, Apollo was the god of light, reason, harmony, balance and prophesy, while Dionysus was the god of wine, revelry, ecstatic emotion and tragedy.

In the twentieth century, some authors took these ideas and started to criticise the mentality of modernity for trying to reduce everything to facts and objective truths that cannot be doubted or questioned. Today, we are living in a time that tries to overcome modernity, and hence the name 'post-modernity.' The concepts of 'post-truth' and 'post-factual' are part of this post-modern movement. This new way of thinking follows the theory initiated by Nietzsche when he declared that *'There are no facts, only interpretations'*.

Post-modern French authors like Michel Foucault (1926–1984) or Jacques Derrida (1930–2004) had an enormous influence on post-modernism, They first started to gain notoriety in academic settings and then in society in general. They managed to give a voice to previously marginalised groups like women, homosexuals, ethnic minorities, people with mental problems, etc. These groups had been excluded by too narrow a concept of 'truth', associated with scientific objectivity.

In post-modern thought, 'truth' is no longer something absolute as it was during the Modern Age. Now, truth is considered to be the most convenient story (or narrative) to the dominant power. There are always institutions with the capacity to establish certain truths associated with a particular power. During the old age it was the Church and the Monarchy. In our society, the institutions imposing those truths are schools, hospitals, prisons, courts of justice, universities, mental institutions, etc. They are the ones in charge of establishing who is normal and who is not, what is true and what is false, what is good and what is bad, what is knowledge and what is superstition, and so on.

If we change the agents of power (the rulers), then the truths and institutions that sustain the system will change too. This assumes that if the conditions are met for it, 'alternative truths' could be presented with equal validity. Only from a dominant power can truth be established, or what is the same: there is no truth without power. The bottom line is that something is true for a limited time only. If truth is not reinforced and defended with states, universities, armies, churches, schools, etc., it will be substituted by some other 'competing truths'. Let's take the example of Iran.

Before the Islamic revolution of 1979, Iran was a fairly liberal country with a Westernised ruling class. After the revolution led by Ayatollah Khomeini, an Iranian political and religious leader who served as the first supreme leader of Iran from 1979, the country came under the control of the clerics and the Shia interpretation of Islam. University courses were Islamised and disciplines such as 'Islamic medicine', 'Islamic sociology' and 'Islamic psychology' were taught. In the Iranian New Year's message, Khomeini himself defined his purpose as follows:

A fundamental revolution should take place in universities all over Iran so that professors who are affiliated with the East or West are purged and universities become healthy environments for teaching advanced Islamic sciences.

But not only were the 'Western academic truths' changed by others of an Islamic nature, the 'legal truths' or conventions of the moment were also disrupted. From then on, the legal age of marriage for women was set at 9 years old, according to Islamic law. Since 1981, adultery was to be be punished with the death penalty by stoning. Women would take the back seats on buses while the front seats were reserved for men. And the legal testimony of a woman was worth half that of a man. In short, new truths were established that were supported by a new power, the Iranian Islamic clergy and the guardians of the revolution.

There is another basic concept of the Modern Age that is currently under attack in post-modern societies: dualism, or in other words 'binary thinking'. We tend to think of the world as a combination of opposites: male/female, left/right, life/death, truth/lies, rational/irrational, rich/poor, body/soul, good/bad, etc. In this dual thinking, one of the two is always the dominant element, and the other one is the dominated. The radical change of post-modernism is that in reality, there is no solid basis that justifies this situation. Males and females, rich people and poor people, left-wing and right-wing, etc., are not essences that are impossible to change. In a post-modern society, it is more appropriate to speak of fluidity between the two extremes. Actually, post-modern thinking prefers to refer to any dualism as a dynamic spectrum. There are no big and solid truths, only small and liquid ones. The truth is not monolithic or a mere description of facts because *there are no objective facts, only interpretations.*

In any case, although the times we live in may seem confusing, it would be unfair to put the blame on post-modern philosophers alone. Their theories have been badly used to justify all sort of things, something that was far from their initial intentions.

Truth and lies

Lies are evil, and truths are good. This is the judgement that has dominated traditional thinking for ages. For many people today, 'post-truth' is simply a way of lying, and therefore it is morally wrong. However, lies, deception, dissimulation, camouflage, etc., are a constant in the animal world, but much more so among humans, because of language. When Nietzsche or Steve Tesich criticised post-truth for being a selective and sugar-coated truth, they did not necessarily want to eliminate lying and deception from reality. They simply wanted us to be aware that lying is also part of our reality. People lie, and that is also part of 'the truth'.

Niccolò Machiavelli (Santi de Tito, S. XVI).

Lying has been (and continues to be) a very important tool for states and politicians. History is full of examples, and one of the best authors to write about it was Niccolò Machiavelli (1469–1527). In his book *The Prince*, he affirms that private and public morality are two different things. Therefore, a ruler should not have scruples in using lies to achieve the best for the state. According to Machiavelli, '*The end justifies the means*', and if one has to use lies and give them the form of truth, it should not be a problem. The goal is always to maintain the authority of a ruler and preserve the stability of the state. Today we use the adjective 'Machiavellian' to describe such practices, but they are more widespread than we want to admit. Facts can only be judged after seeing their consequences. For Machiavelli, a ruler has to be willing to go to Hell for the good of the state. That includes lying or even killing enemies, whenever necessary if there is a greater good at stake. In Machiavelli's words:

For a long time I have not said what I believe, nor do I ever believe what I say, and if indeed I happen to tell the truth, I hide it among so many lies that it is difficult to find.

Machiavelli did not write for the man in the street but for rulers, kings and political leaders. It would not be justified for anyone else to lie or cheat in order to pursue their goals. In recent times, Vladimir Putin would fit perfectly for this kind of ruler.

However, there is a new version of Machiavelli's theory, something that we could say is the post-modern version of Machiavellism. Today, it is not reserved exclusively for states or very powerful individuals to lie and cheat. On the contrary, deceiving and lying are justified to any individual with access to social media (or dating applications, for that matter). In terms of public information, we cannot ignore that some mass media are subjected to 'digital capitalism', which values the number of 'clicks' more than the veracity of the information. They can use lies, deception, confusion or any other strategy that helps in achieving their ideological, economic or political objectives. Reformulating Machiavelli's phrase to adapt it to the current situation: *The number of clicks justifies the means.*

Conclusion

It would be too difficult in practice to accept that there are no truths. To navigate complex societies like ours, we need a map that helps us know the territory. In addition to this map, we need a compass that indicates North if we are to orient ourselves. However, it could be that the needle in other societies indicates a different direction. There is just no single North, although we tend to think that the North of our society is the right one.

Truths have a similar role in our lives. They help us to position ourselves, although sometimes the paradigm changes, and the needle in our compass points to a different direction.

If we understand the world as the totality of phenomena (everything that we know plus the things that we ignore), there is nothing in this world that is 'the truth'. The idea of truth is only a useful and effective way in which humans organise what we already know. For example, it might be true that I weigh 75 kg if the number 75 appears on the screen when I get on a precision scale. However, there is nothing in nature that is 'a kilogram'. It is simply a reference to organise our world and therefore it has a very important practical function. It could be that in another system, I weigh 165.34 pounds or

11.8 stones. The three measures are 'the truth', but it is a truth taken as a reference, not an absolute truth.

In some countries (such as the two Koreas), a baby is considered to be one year old at the time of birth. Also, age increases from the last day of the year, not from one's birthday. If a baby is born on 31st of December, they will be one year old, but they will be two years old the next day even though they have only spent two days alive. In both cases, the truth about a person's age varies depending on the reference we have. In one instance, it corresponds to the number of calendar years that a person has lived. In most countries, age is connected to the number of turns the Earth has made around the sun during a lifetime.

Not having any compass at all and completely abandoning the notion of truth is something that does not make any sense. The truth is a reference, a needle that points North. However, we could be favourably inclined to admit that post-truth is the explicit recognition that there are other valid ways of organising our knowledge of the world.

It could well be that the colour red of a traffic light means that we can cross the road and that the green light tells us to stop. In reality, there is nothing in the colour red itself that prohibits us from crossing. However, a traffic light cannot be interpretable, otherwise we would be in trouble.

Many of the changes in our societies in recent years are given not by the fact that 'red' means 'green', but because red and green can mean many different (and sometimes contradictory) things. This is undoubtedly the cause of much of the confusion that we see in our time and the frustration that it generates.

The only thing that is undebatable here is that in recent years, post-truth has conquered a territory that was previously exclusive of 'big truths'. The Modern Age is becoming post-modern.

CHAPTER 3

DEMOCRACY: IS THERE
AN ALTERNATIVE?

'Democracy is the worst form of government,
except for all the others.'
(Winston Churchill)

Discussion

We tend to assume that democracy is without any possible discussion, that it is the best way of governing our societies. However, our ideas about democracy have changed a good deal throughout history. Are there real and acceptable alternatives? Is democracy unquestionable in the same manner as some religions are perceived to be? What valid arguments are given for and against democracy? What could we expect from democracy in the future? Can we say that democracy is in real danger?

Introduction

If we take a look at a map of the world today, we will find some rather peculiar states whose size and population are extremely small. In some cases, their extension is limited to a few square miles. Monaco, San Marino, Andorra, Liechtenstein, Bahrain or Singapore are all sovereign and independent countries. However, if they want to have any chance of survival, given their minuscule size, they have to seek alliances to protect themselves and find trade partners to do business with.

In the fourth and fifth centuries BC, classical Greece functioned in many ways like those tiny countries of today. It was a conglomerate of fairly independent city-states and for some time, the city-state of Athens was the most splendid of them all. Outstanding in the cultural and intellectual field, it was governed by a democratic political system of direct participation. It was, without a doubt, one of the best places in the world to live in those days (if you were not a slave).

During the Athenian spring of 399 BC, a very famous trial was held. It was so important that it has been acknowledged as a crucial event in the course of the history of Western civilisation. This trial has been described by writers, analysed by philosophers, painted by artists, etc. Its influence has been such that it is still relevant today, almost 2,500 years later.

It took place in the hill of Pnyx, where the Athenians used to gather to talk on political issues, and to take decisions on the future of their town. The jury consisted of 500 people, all male. Every one of them had been chosen randomly among those who volunteered. The money paid for fulfilling their role was not huge, but they all received a minimum payment for their attendance and participation during the trial. In front of this jury, a 70-year-old man appeared as defendant. He had been described as short and not very handsome. He had bulging eyes, a flat nose, a large mouth and full lips. He was accused of two crimes, and both of them were very serious: impiety and moral corruption. The prosecution requested the death penalty for this old man responsible for the charges.

The death of Socrates (Jacques-Louis David 1787).

Impiety was a crime that consisted of denying the existence of the official gods. It was said that by having his own gods the accused was disrespecting the traditions of the city of Athens. The other charge he had to face was that of morally corrupting the young Athenians. Following the teachings of this old man, the youngsters rebelled against their parents and the traditional morality of the city. This is strikingly reminiscent of another famous trial in history in which a 33-year-old Jesus was accused of similar crimes. Questioning the authorities, was a dangerous thing because it endangered the entire social

and political fabric of Athens. During the trial, the defendant
was described as:

*'...a certain intellectual, meditator of celestial phenomena, and
who says that everything that is under the earth he has investigat-
ed, and that he defends lost causes and makes white look black.'*

*The Academy of Athens, with Plato and Aristotle in the centre
(Raphael 1509–1510).*

If this seemingly crazy man were allowed to continue his
dangerous teachings, or they permitted him to question everything, or even if they allowed him to examine all their knowledge in a rational manner, they would run the risk of breaking
the pillars on which the city was based. Uh, uh, they will not
let this happen!

This old man was Socrates, and he knew that his chances of being found innocent were very slim. When the jury found him guilty, the worst expectations were confirmed: it was the death penalty. However, there was still a silver lining as capital punishment could be commuted to permanent exile. If Socrates agreed to leave Athens, never to return, he would preserve his life. Some of his friends breathed a sigh of relief, but those who had been in close contact with Socrates knew that he would rather drink hemlock, a poison that would end his life in a matter of minutes. To do otherwise would have been humiliating to him. Being kicked out of the city in which he had grown up and in which he had become such a popular character was not an option. Besides, walking into exile meant accepting that he had done something wrong. That was not the case and Socrates preferred death rather than renouncing his principles.

Accompanying him throughout the process was a young disciple who was deeply shocked by the outcome of the trial, as well as being stunned by Socrates' decision to accept the death penalty. This young man was the philosopher Plato (427–347 BC), and he watched with horror how 280 of the 500 jurors (56% of them) voted against his innocence. Plato wondered who these men were and why they were allowed to do such a thing. What authority or superior knowledge did they claim in order to judge the old master of Athens? Did they really know who Socrates was and the kind of things that he was teaching? No, obviously not. How was it possible that the political system of the city could be this unfair? It did not make sense that a simple majority system could decide on the life of this wise man. He, who had taught so many things to the people of Athens. What about the opinion of the other 220 people who considered Socrates innocent?

Enemies of democracy

From that very moment, Plato became a declared enemy of a cruel system (democracy) that had condemned an innocent man through an unfair decision. Plato's opinion was that the ignorant were condemning the wise, and this could not be tolerated. It was the world upside down.

The Republic, without a doubt one of Plato's most famous books, explains in detail the political theory of the author. He did not believe that democracy was the most appropriate form of government. Clearly, in the name of democracy, injustices are committed, and no one is held responsible for them. There is no accountability in democracy. Besides, in Athens, one could buy votes and easily corrupt the system. In a democracy the ignorant have the same decision-making power as the educated. In order to avoid these political deficiencies in an ideal republic, Plato proposed to eliminate the democratic system. Instead, he believed that they had to create the right conditions to educate an elite of rulers. Ideally, this elite would not be corrupted by power, or money or material possessions. They would exclusively dedicate themselves to the work of government. The perfect political system would be a republic ruled by an elite of civil servants, technocrats and officials whose main objective in their lives was the creation of a fair and efficient state. At the head of this republic, there would be a leader, a wise person, a philosopher, someone who probably would not want to rule. However, this person should be persuaded to do so since their refusal to take power only confirms their suitability as a leader.

Plato was suspicious of professional politicians who wanted to govern for the wrong reasons: money, power, influence, fame, etc. He did not believe in the democratic system because of its tendency to respect only the appetites of the masses. He thought that in democracies most citizens didn't really under-stand the law, and they didn't listen to the experts. For Plato, the essence of democracy was a mass of individuals who con-sidered themselves experts in anything when in reality they were not, and the worst thing of all was that they were not willing to learn from those who really knew.

The great philosopher Aristotle (384–322 BC) did not get to know Socrates, but when he moved to Athens, he was educated by Plato in his school 'The Academy', founded in the gardens dedicated to the Greek god Academus (and hence the origin of the word ‹academy› that we continue to use today). Perhaps it was the influence of his master, but Aristotle did not consider himself to be especially fond of democracy either. He simply said that it was one of several forms of government that may exist, but nothing else. Democracy is not intrinsically superior, or better, than any other fair form of governing the '*polis*' (the city-state). Characteristically, Aristotle made a very smart clas-sification of the potential forms of government. He used the number of rulers and fairness as criteria for his distinction.

'Monarchy' would be the government of one single person if the monarch is fair, but if this king is unfair, it would be a 'tyranny'.

The government of a few people will be considered an 'aris-tocracy' if it is a fair one, but 'oligarchy' if it is unfair.

Finally, the government of many people could be called 'democracy' (or republic) when it is fair, but 'demagogy' if it is corrupt.

Number of Rulers	Fair government	Unfair government
One ruler	Monarchy	Tyranny
Few rulers	Aristocracy	Oligarchy
Many rulers	Democracy	Demagogy

Aristotle was not neutral and clearly took sides. He preferred the monarchy as the most perfect form to rule a state. At the same time, he admitted that it was also the most difficult government because finding a fair monarch was extremely rare. If it were not possible to find the right person to be the supreme legislator, they would have to consider other possibilities. Only then could democracy be an option.

Old democracies and democracy today

Once we have reached this point, it would be necessary to question whether the idea of democracy in ancient Greece was the same that we have today. Did they understand 'democracy' to be the same thing as now?

In fact, 'democracy' is an idea that has evolved throughout history and has come down to us quite distorted from its origin, given its multiple modulations. We can talk about democracy in different areas, for example: in politics, in business, in a book club, in a family, etc. In each context, 'democracy' would be understood differently.

What seems to be clearer is the technical procedure in our political system. Among other things it includes: voting, majorities, political parties, universal suffrage, electoral campaigns, debates, coalitions, etc. A democratic country, therefore, is one that follows this technical process and makes sure that all the boxes are ticked: free elections, universal votes, equal rights, etc.

However, it is easy to point at a particular problem here. If we use our democratic system as criteria, we would have great difficulty accepting as 'democratic' any society in which only a small group of people have access to vote. In classical Athens, the percentage of individuals entitled to vote was considerably lower than those who could not, yet Athens is considered to be a model of democracy. Even if we analyse more recent examples of democracy, such as the United States in the eighteenth century, nobody will accept it today as a real democracy, especially because of the maintenance of a slave society. What kind of democratic society today would tolerate this? This, nonetheless, was the reference only some decades ago, but does this mean that until now there have been no real democracies? And what if in the future we look back to our society and we discover that prisoners, foreigners or people under 18 were not allowed to vote? Could it be said that we were not fully democratic?

Things do not really get better if we examine some democracies of the twentieth century in Europe. We do not see clear examples of what we understand as 'democracy' today. Can we say that a country is democratic when women cannot vote? Definitively not with our standards of democracy. Women were not able to vote until quite recently, even in countries that we consider to be 'full democracies'. France granted the right for women to vote in 1944 and Liechtenstein only in 1984. Other countries declared themselves to be 'democratic', but in reality, they were dictatorships masked under the name of 'democracies'. The German Democratic Republic was actually a communist dictatorship until after 1989 as it was under the influence of the Soviet Union. Others, like the Democratic Republic of Congo is not necessarily a good example of what we understand for 'democratic' if we use our standards of today.

In our day, democracy is considered to be a superior political system. Many people seems to have a very simplistic historical account of democracy. They believe that democracy appears as a diamond discovered in classical Greece but soon forgotten during the Roman Empire. The Middle and the Modern Ages (with some exceptions like the city-states of Switzerland or the Netherlands) did not appreciate the democratic system in its fair measure and they preferred repressive and strongly hierarchical political systems. The story goes that the Americans 'rescued' democracy from oblivion in the eighteenth century, and since then, it has been expanding until we reached the liberal capitalist democracies of today. Whether in a conscious manner or not, most people in the West consider these liberal democracies the brightest moment in the evolution of politics.

After centuries of challenges, the democratic system proved to be a supreme value. It is commonly seen as the most refined political form that has ever been and will ever be. All its alternatives have proven inferior, or to put it in the words of Winston Churchill (1874–1965), democracy is *the worst form of government except for all the others that have been used'*.

Democracy and the end of History

Francis Fukuyama (1952) has the air of an educated and serious man. He has advised several Presidents of the United States and he is a respected intellectual with numerous publications on international politics. His surname suggests a Japanese background but despite having a cosmopolitan education in New York, he did not learn Japanese from his parents, nor was he very close to Japanese culture. Instead, he was much more interested in politics and philosophy. During his college years he travelled to Paris to study for 6 months and there, he came into contact with the radical ideas coming from the French academy (that of Barthes, Foucault and Derrida specifically). However, Fukuyama grew quite disappointed with post-modern philosophy and focused on political studies. In 1989 he wrote a very influential article entitled: *The End of History?* He later expanded his thesis into a book of the same name that was a spectacular success. It is regularly cited to this day even though his ideas were also harshly criticized for having a too naive and pro-Western perspective.

Fukuyama thought that we had reached the end of history. Seeing all possible options, capitalist liberal democracies were the only possible alternative. They had proved to be vastly superior to other systems. All other alternative political ideologies had been exhausted after the fall of the Soviet Union and the end of the communist utopia. The market economy had replaced many political regimes in the Western world, and sooner or later, the population would demand a transition to liberal democracy.

Despite the criticism that his argument caused, Fukuyama's theory was developed at a time when the world was no longer divided into two: the communist bloc and the-capitalist democracies. It seemed that the fight had been won by the latter and that there was no opponent worthy of offering a viable alternative. The Soviet Union had disintegrated into several countries that were gradually making the transition to more democratic systems and market economies. China at that time, although still a communist country, was too far behind in terms of economy as well as technology, it was seen as a poor backward country that offered no clear alternative. If anything, after[7] policy, the country was adopting a hybrid

---

7. Dent Xiaoping was a Chinese revolutionary leader, military commander and statesman who served as the paramount leader of the People's Republic of China

system between communism and capitalism that some have called 'state capitalism'. China started to adopt a more pragmatic view and the country was ready to turn the page on the ideological purity of Mao. Deng Xiaoping summed up this new policy in these terms: *'No matter if it is a white cat or a black cat. As long as it catches the mice is a good cat'*. The success of this state capitalism in both Russia and China has greatly increased their international relevance and today they seriously compete with the United States and the European Union.

By the time Fukuyama published his article it could be argued that history was dead. However, Russia and China have resurrected it. In 2014, China became the world's largest economy and Russia has created a new iron curtain with the West with the invasion of territories that once belonged to the Soviet Union.

As it turns out, it has not been the end of history, far from it. Rather, it seems that history, understood as the struggle of powers for control, has been asleep for an unusually long period (about 30 years or so) and has now woken up again. After the invasion of Ukraine in February 2022, with Vladimir Putin at the head of the Russian state, a new antagonism is established against Western liberal democracies. It is today impossible to speak of the end of history, the alliance of civilizations or a 'perpetual peace' (paraphrasing Kant). In this period of relative calm, some European Union states barely invested their budget in weapons or military development. This clearly

---

(PRC) from December 1978 to November 1989. After Chinese Communist Party chairman Mao Zedong's death in 1976, Deng gradually rose to supreme power and led China through a series of far-reaching market-economy reforms earning him the reputation as the "Architect of Modern China". He contributed to China becoming the world's second largest economy by GDP nominal in 2010.

shows that Fukuyama was not alone in thinking that we had achieved a permanent new world order.

This belief that our current political system is the best (liberal democracies) is not a new thing. Fukuyama is influenced by the ideas of the philosopher Georg Wilhem Friedrich Hegel (1770–1831) born in Stuttgart, which at that time was part of Prussia. Hegel considered that the Prussian state in which he lived represented the ultimate political evolution in history. The reforms introduced in Prussia, such as a new school system, granting citizenship to Jews, abolishing serfdom and establishing free trade, made Hegel believe that his state was the best that ever existed in history. Prussia was at the time the cream of the crop.

It is also relevant to mention Karl Marx (1818–1883). He was arguably the most influential political thinker of the last two centuries, and he also was a disciple of Hegel. They both had a very similar idea regarding history. Since the beginning of humanity there has been an evolution from worse to better. This evolution is not peaceful since there is constantly a struggle between opposites that generate a new situation, and this is how history progresses. One of the great differences between Hegel and Marx is that for Marx we had not yet arrived at the most perfect form of government. We were close, though, and according to him, all the conditions were met in order to take the final step. We were so close that we only needed one revolution to reach the true social justice: the communist paradise. In some of his writings Marx considers democracy as a bourgeois concept that needs to be overcome.

Although these theories might seem strange to us today, it should not be overlooked that our opinion of the current democratic system is similar to that of Hegel, Marx and Fukuyama. It is as if all the problems in the world could be solved with more democracy. Besides, we can find abundant examples of 'democratic fundamentalism' in which democracy is seen almost as a religion. The constitution would be the holy book and the politicians are the modern equivalent to the religious clergy. If there are deficiencies in democracies, the system is not to blame because the democratic system is perfect itself. Corrupt politicians are the ones to blame (just as Luther saw the corruption of the Catholic clergy). Under this narrow view, it is not about adjusting the system to society, but rather adjusting society to the system, because democracy is perfect and societies are not. Politicians, political parties, voters, the media… all of them are wrong and responsible for distorting the 'sacred' democratic procedure.

Adolf Hitler came to power after democratic elections.

Many times we fall into the naivety of thinking that if a country adopts a liberal democratic system, there will be no turning back, nor will there be an alternative that can compete with it. It is the end of History (with a capital letter), but surely not the end of 'history' (with lower case) because, local historical events will continue to happen.

But who in their right mind could question the superiority of our democratic system? It would be sacrilege, a manoeuvre by morally degenerate individuals who want to destroy the well-being that has been built over so many years and with so much effort. Nobody would be allowed to doubt it, but in fact there are alternatives to democracy as we know it today. These alternatives, when argued rationally, are worthy of being considered in a serious and honest debate. Let's not condemn Socrates again.

Several commentators believe that it is possible to alter our current political system if we want to make it more efficient and more in line with the needs of our society. There is of course a price to pay, and it does not seem that the majority could be in favour of paying it.

Restricted democracy

Jason Brennan (1979) is a philosopher and academic from the United States who, like Plato in the fifth century BC., does not agree with the current democratic system. His reasons for that are also similar. In his 2016 book, *Against Democracy*, he argues that it would not be appalling to conceive a system in which there are limits to the decision-making power of people deemed irrational, incompetent or ignorant. At first glance, almost everyone would agree with this idea, but it raises a bigger problem: who can decide who is a 'competent or incompetent' person? In what seems to be an exercise in naivety, Brennan believes that people should be honest with themselves and with the system. If they really believe that they are not ready to vote, then they have a moral obligation to abstain. In his opinion, a good alternative to democracy would be 'epistocracy'. Epistocracy is a system in which those who can demonstrate their political knowledge have a greater specific weight in decision-making. Brennan explains this situation with the following words:

We know that an unfortunate side effect of democracy is that it incentivizes citizens to be ignorant, irrational, tribalistic, and to not use their votes in very serious ways. So this is an attempt to correct for that pathology while keeping what's good about a democratic system. We have to ask ourselves what we think government is actually for. Some people think it has the value a painting has, which is to say that it's symbolic. In that view, you might think, "We should have democracy because it's a way of civilizing and expressing the idea that all of us have equal value." There's another way of looking at government, which is that it's a tool, like a hammer, and the purpose of politics is to generate just and good outcomes, to generate efficiency and stability, and to avoid mistreating people. So if you think government is for that purpose, and I do, then you have to wonder if we should pick the form of government that best delivers the goods, whatever that might be.

Democracy is generally seen as a supreme good, but it is no surprise that most of our institutions: schools, hospitals, businesses, families, churches, universities, etc., are not democratic themselves. They work perfectly in an *'undemocratic'* way, and very few would be convinced to send their children to a *'democratic school'* or enter a *'democratic hospital'*. Some may argue: Why should a state be different? Already in the nineteenth century, the British politician and economist John Stuart Mill (1806–1873) asked that those with university degrees, or those who carried out intellectual jobs, should have more weight in the decision-making of their government.

Brennan is not alone when he states that voting is not a simple right. It is not a dowry that one receives at birth but rather a privilege that requires effort. Therefore, it would be necessary to prove by means of a test or some other sophisticated procedure that a citizen has appropriate knowledge of the system and the functioning of the state in which they live. If it is necessary to pass an exam to obtain the right to drive, the same should be done to acquire the right to vote. Many countries are using similar requirements for foreigners if they want to become citizens, they need to pay an amount of money, prove that they are not convicted criminals, demonstrate their language skills and pass a knowledge test. Then, and only then, can they be full citizens.

All this intellectual opposition to democracy (as we know it today) is based on the idea that citizens are not trained well enough to make decisions on important and complex matters such as labour market reform, tax collection, pensions, membership of the European Union, the independence of a territory, etc.

Among defenders of democracy there seems to be a kind of fixation with the idea of voting in elections, as if democracy were reduced to that. In some countries like Iran, you can also vote and elect candidates for the presidency, but that is not enough to consider Iran a fully democratic country. On the other hand, in societies considered fully democratic, there is always a part of the population that cannot exercise their right to vote, such as minors, intellectually disabled people, some prisoners and foreigners residing in the country. This, however, does not mean that their other rights are affected.

Other arguments against democracy

Brennan's argument is not the only one against democracy as there are many others. For instance, it has been criticised on numerous occasions that the dynamics of political parties in a democracy tend to divide society (often artificially and unnecessarily). Different social groups are already divisive enough, and we do not need to confront them even further over issues that are not always relevant. Democracy, coupled with partisan media, would generate conflicts rather than resolve them. In recent years we have seen how the societies of democratic countries fragmented into apparently irreconcilable groups. The most obvious example in recent times is the referendum for the UK to leave the European Union. During the campaign and especially after the result, it generated a division and a social climate of tension that did not exist previously. However, today we live in times in which the polarization generated by the prospect of a democratic election is the norm in many countries. The United States, Italy, Brazil, Hungary, etc. are just examples of this.

Democracy does not seem to be the most effective political system either. The continuous consultations to the population (or the congress) means that projects are delayed. They also block necessary reforms and affect the quality of life of many citizens. On the contrary, other non-democratic states are much more dynamic and effective in responding to the needs of the population[8]. It would not be absurd to think that in the future, these

---

8. Prusia in he 19th century or China today are examples of this kind of states.

states will have greater power in the international arena, and in fact, some of them already form a serious alternative to democratic powers. History also leaves us with innumerable examples of states that have enjoyed enormous material and cultural success without committing themselves to *democratic principles*.

Finally, democracy would have to face another weighty argument: the majority. Majorities do not always choose what is most fair or what is best for society (unless we accept that 'fair' is only what the majority chooses). It seems that the only rationality that we could find in democracy is its own formal structure. The way democracy works is rational but that rationality is not extended to its theoretical principles. Democratic values are not necessarily clear or rational in themselves. In other words, there is no theoretical way to show that democracies are better (or worse) than other possible systems of government. It is simply a matter of preference and the idea of what a good outcome would look like. If the objective is to maintain a population of hundreds of millions in a permanent state of social stability in which values such as family or respect for traditions are the dominant ones, perhaps a democratic regime is not the best. Electing the politicians who will form parliament every four or five years will not solve more problems than other forms of government. In fact, it will create other problems unique to that system (vote buying, inefficiency, bureaucracy, demagogy, etc.).

Advocates of democracy

On the other hand, it seems clear that the arguments in favour of our democratic system are many. For example, in democratic countries, famines do not normally occur. Democratic countries normally do not declare war on other democratic countries. They do not kill their own citizens (although, in some places, the death penalty is still in force). In democratic countries, transitions of power are normally peaceful, and there is respect for the physical integrity of its citizens and their freedom of expression. All of these traits are difficult to find in other non-democratic systems.

With these arguments alone, one could be entitled to be a fervent defender of democracy, no matter its deficiencies. However, those who are critical of the idea of democracy as a superior form of government, assure us that it is possible to have an alternative system where these positive features are maintained. Democracy in itself does not contain any superior values. These positive attributes could be preserved in an alternative system. In summary, opposing today's democracy does not mean advocating for a military dictatorship, defending a communist state or supporting fascist regimes.

The future of democracy

There is no reason to believe either that countries with democratic governments will remain unchanged, nor that citizens will fight and resist any attempt to change that form of government. As we know, everything is temporary, and nothing is permanent. Political regimes are no exception.

It could be argued that countries are democratic only because they can afford to be so. They will cease to be democratic as soon as they cannot afford to be democratic anymore. In other words, democracies are sustained by certain material conditions such as: access to mineral resources, energy supplies, military defence of borders, access to markets for their products, climatic conditions, etc. If these material conditions change to a certain degree, their political system will have to do the same. Democracy, in its actual form, would no longer be valid. A very recent example is the situation experienced in most countries during the Covid-19 lockdowns. The material conditions at that time were so different that democracy (with its freedom of association, freedom of movement, etc.), was replaced by a much more restrictive model: curfew, labour restrictions, limitation in the purchase of products, etc. Those measures were considered to be more appropriate to face the situation, but they were certainly not very democratic.

In many ways, our idea of democracy is shaped by the economic system we live in (market capitalism), where everything, or almost everything, can be chosen. Consumers in such societies expect to be able to choose everything in their lives, from the colour of their cars to the brand of coffee they drink every morning. In this constant decision-making, marketing and advertising play a great role. Decisions that at first glance seem like a 'free choice', are actually influenced by many other factors that condition them. Something very similar would happen in our political decisions. We should be able to choose, as if we were in a supermarket, all 'democratic items': the politicians, the political parties, policies, etc.

Many political parties, in order to make their manifestos more attractive, use techniques similar to those employed in marketing when they try to sell any other consumer product. As electoral bait, politicians use in their speeches and public events: television commercials, promises of cash back, pension raises, tax breaks, free services, celebrity supporters, use of influencers, etc.

In reality, our options are more limited than they seem at first glance. Our political choices are driven by other factors that are not always obvious, such as demographics, the state of the economy or advertising campaigns.

Conclusion

Democracy in our time is more than just a political idea, it is also a moral concept. We tend to think that if something is 'democratic', it is automatically 'good' or 'fair'. However, it does not seem logical to think that what the majority chooses is always the best or the fairest. Plato could not find anything fair in the decision of the majority condemning Socrates. We don't have to think too hard to find instances in which decisions taken by democratic means have had dire results.

Actually, there are very few aspects of life that are really democratic. Children in a school cannot democratically decide the menu as they most likely would eat sweets and pasta. Parents have to 'undemocratically forced' them to eat fruit and vegetables. Similarly, the workers of a company cannot democratically decide their wages or the number of weeks they can take off work.

We run the risk of seeing democracy as a dogma that does not admit any criticism. Although it may seem like a contradiction, one can criticise the democratic system and be a democrat at the same time because democracy is not an essence. We should avoid the temptation of distinguishing between democratic and non-democratic countries because democracy is a spectrum. Athens was a democracy but not in the same way as we understand democracy now.

Furthermore, there is not just one type of democratic system, as each country has different rules. For example, in Australia or Brazil, voting is mandatory, not optional. It's actually quite an undemocratic idea, but that's not saying that those countries are dictatorships.

It should be the role of philosophers and 'intellectuals' to draw the limits of what can be done and said in the name of democracy (or any other idea for the same reason). Otherwise, we will easily fall into fundamentalism in the name of a greater good.

CHAPTER 4

LEFT AND RIGHT

'The right is dissolved in the left.
It's the left but with another name.'

(Gustavo Bueno)

Discussion

We seem to act as if we have a very clear idea of what it means to
be left-wing or right-wing. However, evidence shows that this is
not the case and confusion prevails. What does it mean to be left-
wing? Is it the same as being liberal or progressive? Is it the same
everywhere? What do we mean by being right-wing, then? Is it not
possible to be a leftist and conservative at the same time? Do these
terms have the same meaning as in the nineteenth or twentieth
century? What is more, can we say that this dualism is still valid
for such a complex post-modern society like ours?

Introduction

'O God, guide us, protect us! We are too young to reign.' With this prayer, Louis Capet knelt when he learned that his grandfather had died, and he was becoming Louis XVI, the new King of France.

He was 20 years old and despite having received a good education, when it came time to rule, he felt utterly lost and did not know what to do and how to act. Actually, he had not been born with the idea that he would be the Dauphin, that is, the natural heir to the throne of France. His older brother, considered by all to be the most attractive and intelligent, died at the tender age of nine and the situation changed completely. Although cultured and able to speak in several languages he was too shy and indecisive, lacking the qualities of a strong leader. These reasons partly explain how he came to his end, at the age of 39, publicly beheaded for betraying the French people.

At the age of fifteen, he married the Austrian Archduchess Marie Antoinette, who was only 14. Initially she made a good impression among the people but, actually, she was never very popular in France because she was considered a foreigner from an enemy country. In addition, during the first eight years of marriage she did not produce an heir to the throne and that worried everyone. Rumours circulated that something strange was happening because the couple had not even consummated their marriage.

Despite much speculation, the reason had been kept secret by the King for all these years. His erections caused him enormous pain that prevented him from having sexual relations. Once he made it known to his doctors, and with a simple phimosis operation (an intervention destined to remove the foreskin of the penis), the problem was solved and several heirs to the throne were born. However, rumours spread among the people about the legitimacy of the children and Marie Antoinette was accused of being a promiscuous woman, wasteful and an enemy of France. Actually, it was more a question about the extravagance of the Court. The sumptuous parties at Versailles had gone too far and she was known by the name of 'Madame Deficit'. All this things together did not help the people of France to have a good opinion of their royal family.

Young Louis XVI (Antoine-François Callet, 1786).

In the summer of 1789, however, the King still retained the support of his subjects despite widespread discontent over the economic crisis, high food prices, poor harvests and high taxes to pay for wars. Let us not forget the opulent life at the palace that decimated the royal coffers. Over time, the population's patience was wearing thin.

The French people demanded changes and, for the first time in 175 years, Louis was forced to convene the 'Estates General', the representative body of France. At the time of the call, power was distributed in an extremely unbalanced way. The estates of the nobility and the clergy had two-thirds of the power despite representing only 3% of the population. Regardless of whether they were rich or poor, all the common people had to settle for the other third of the vote.

When the lawyer and statesman Maximilien Robespierre (1758–1794), on behalf of the French people, demanded that the nobility and clergy also pay taxes to maintain the war and mitigate the state's bankruptcy, the King reacted angrily. He prevented the commons from making the decisions of power. However, this action ended up confirming a serious miscalculation. As a form of protest, the *Commune* ("the common people") formed the 'National Constituent Assembly'. It was an alternative power that tried to change the unjust situation that had been maintained until that very moment. The Assembly declared itself as the true representative of the French people, something that was new in France. After several well-known revolts, such as the storming of the Bastille, the Assembly declared that all citizens were equal and demanded that the King's power be limited and subjected to the will of the population, as was the case in the English monarchy.

In a very important vote celebrated on August 1789 it was decided whether or not the King had the right of veto. The monarch was seated in the centre of the room; to his right were the moderates and the monarchists. These were known as the 'Girondins' and were in favour of the King's power of veto. To his left were those who opposed royal privileges and were in favour of the political and social changes of the revolution. On this side were the *petite bourgeoisie* (middle and upper-middle classes) and the rest of the people of France.

Confusing terms

This spatial division between left and right has since acquired a political dimension. However, it cannot be said that these terms are as clear today as they were at that time, especially when there are no absolute kings in the West and no political party supports privileges by any establishment (or at least not openly).

In August 2019 the British market research and data analytics firm 'YouGov' published a survey which perfectly exemplifies the confusion in which we live regarding the meaning of 'left' and 'right'. In this survey, 28% of those asked declared themselves to be leftists, 25% to be right-wing supporters, while 19% considered themselves in the centre. The rest of the respondents (28%) did not place themselves in any position or did not understand what was meant by the concepts 'left' and 'right'.

Of those who declared themselves on the right, 57% believed that the state should play a significant or dominant role in the economy. Even 47% of them would approve a nationalisation of the railways. One can only think of the reaction of traditional right-wing voters when seeing these proposals since those are policies traditionally associated with the left. Historically, these interventionist policies have been totally rejected by right-wing voters for fear of falling into a socialist regime dominated by a state that is too strong and able to control all aspects of citizens' lives.

Estates General in Versailles in 1789.

Faced with this confusing ideological scenario, could we affirm that the concepts of 'left' and 'right' are still valid in Western capitalist democracies of the twenty-first century?

Relevance of the terms

If we consider historical figures like Confucius, Jesus, Shakespeare or Napoleon, what sense would it make to think of them as ideologically divided between left or right? We would agree to say that those terms are not applicable to these figures since they lived in a very different time in which those concepts did not exist. Then, why assume that the same concepts are valid for us today? The post-modern society in which we live is completely different from that of the nineteenth century and, to a large extent, also from that of the twentieth century. Isn't dividing between 'left' and 'right' rather a reductive dualism that simplifies a more complex and heterogeneous reality?

If in recent times there has been a growing tendency to consider gender (masculine and feminine) as something fluid, wouldn't it also be appropriate to consider our relationship between the two extremes (left and right) as 'fluid'? In this new reality, one does not have to fully identify with one position or another. Each individual can be more or less left-wing or right-wing depending on the topic that we are considering. There are many factors such as age, economic status, profession, family situation, studies or friendships, that influence our political views. Depending on what moment of our lives, we will feel more inclined to one side or the other of the political spectrum. In fact, it is something that happens constantly when we analyse the results of two different elections. There are, almost always, changes in the results and that means that the same people vote for parties with different ideologies depending on the circumstances.

We should not forget that all ideas, including 'left' and 'right', are dynamic and not static. Their meaning changes over time. Ideas can also mean something different in the past and in the future. What is even more interesting is that they can mean different things at the same time to the point of being contradictory. Someone who claims to be left-wing in Venezuela would easily come into conflict with someone who claims to be left-wing in Japan or the United States. It would therefore be impossible to set a left-wing (or right-wing) ideology in which everyone agrees. For example, for many people, being a left-winger means to be opposed to organised religion, or at least to oppose its dogmas; however, we find leftist social movements in Muslim countries, Christian-socialist parties or communist militants in religious institutions.

For others in the West, being a right-winger means a defence of traditional Christian family values. However, what about the large number of homosexuals who vote for right-wing parties? And what of the thousands of women who vote for Catholic parties but who voluntarily decide to terminate their pregnancies against the official position of the church? It all seems contradictory.

All of the above illustrates the slippery ground on which we move when we initiate a political debate between left and right. On many occasions, they are no more than empty terms, unless we clearly specify what type of left or right we refer to. At the moment, and by looking at the way we use the terms, they seem to be words to disqualify rivals. Sometimes they are just sounds without a meaningful content. It is not possible to speak of an ideological unity of the left because the conflict among its factions is constant (the same would happen with the right).

The way we form our political beliefs and take our political decisions is, in many cases, sectarian. It is not uncommon to follow a political party, or a charismatic leader, based on a decision that has not been taken after a rational deliberation. Sometimes, our choices are not grounded on what we think is best for us or our society. What happens in politics, happens in sports; one chooses an option with no criteria other than local implantation, family tradition or even social pressure (the same as a child would pick their football team). Only after, there may be an *ad-hoc* justification for that preference, but the criterion is rarely rational or coherent, as there are many other factors influencing that decision.

Without prejudice to what has been said above and accepting the plurality of positions, it would be possible to give some historical defining features of what 'left' and 'right' stand for. Necessarily, these definitions have to be very general and abstract because the very moment we get into the details, the cracks in the supposed unity of left/right ideology start to become evident.

Equality vs freedom

Broadly speaking, the image that the left and the right have of society (and how this should be) is very different. For the left, society can be taken as a whole, a unit without much regard for the individual, which is why they believe that left-wing politics can be universal. We are all equal, and equality is the central idea of the left. Society is like a Meccano model that can be assembled and disassembled according to a plan. It is possible to form an ideal society with the pieces (the citizens), but first, the individuals need to conform to the plan. To make sure that the citizens comply with that plan, it is necessary to convince them. Hence the important role that education and culture have for the left. Individuals must be persuaded and guided peacefully through education and culture but, if they resist, it will have to be done in a revolutionary way (which normally means using violent methods).

On the other hand, the right does not believe in a single solution or a unique plan that solves universal problems. Rather, it is the individual states with their coercive power, institutions and armies that guarantee the rights of the citizens in those states. For them, there is no such thing as 'universal human rights'; this is seen as a chimera, a great utopia because, de facto, many countries do not comply with them. The right sees society from an organicist[9] point of view, not a mechanis-

---

9. The parts that make up a society are like the organs of the body, they are all different and fulfill a specific function. Not all can be the same.

tic one (like the left does). As a result, there are different social groups that behave like an organism, sometimes fighting
and sometimes collaborating between themselves. The same
would happen in international politics where different states
constantly declare wars and make peace. There is a permanent
fight for resources, for the control of a territory, the leadership
of a community, etc. For a right-wing ideology, there are clear
limits to what can be done in principle. That limit is imposed
by the individual states and the struggle for limited resources. In some ways, right-wing ideology is more pragmatic and
there is no room for utopias. However, some critics on the left
consider this to be a complete hypocrisy since the right has its
own utopias (such as the equilibrium of supply and demand
or the belief in 'an invisible hand' that regulates the markets).

The fundamental concept for the right is not 'equality' but
'individual freedom'. This creates another problem because
the idea of 'freedom', when taken to the extreme, is as utopian and metaphysical as that of the socialist paradise in which
there are no classes or inequalities. There is no such thing as
'absolute freedom'.

However, if we avoid the extremes and consider the idea of
freedom from a 'moderate' perspective, we see that freedom
is something that cannot be given in the abstract. It has to
be a rather limited version of it, and that is how 'freedom'
becomes 'liberties'. States, or other powers, are the ones that
guarantee these liberties, but this is not necessarily freedom
as an abstract idea, it is actually something more tangible and
concrete. Even the least democratic states have to guarantee
certain liberties. In a complex society like ours, 'freedom' can
never be total since every right is linked to some duties or
certain rules that we need to obey, no matter what we think
about them. For example, freedom of expression can never be

total in any state; there are always limits (for instance defama-
tion), although these limits are sometimes diffuse and open to
misunderstandings. The same would happen to our freedom
of movement, freedom of information, etc.

Liberty Leading the People (Delacroix, 1830).

The fundamental difference is that for the right, 'freedom'
is a principle and for the left, 'freedom' is a consequence of
equality; it can only occur after a revolution that seeks to eliminate the differences between individuals. For the left, then,
there is no freedom without equality. For the right there is no
equality if first we do not have freedom.

Left-wing ideologies are normally suspicious of traditional
power institutions that are not egalitarian, such as 'family' or
'religion' (although we have already mentioned that this view
is not shared by many religious people who vote for left-wing
parties). Private property is also seen as a source of inequality,

and hence many left-wing parties prefer communal property or impose high taxes on those who accumulate more. It is for this reason that traditionally left-wing policies have a greater intervention in the economy. It is the responsibility of the state to redistribute wealth. For the right, meanwhile, the state should dedicate itself to guaranteeing a free market. Markets, by themselves, will be in charge of redistributing wealth if there are optimal conditions for it. The duty of a state should be the pursuit of those conditions. However, the question of what 'optimal conditions' means and how to achieve this goal is another complicated debate.

Inevitably, any political ideology is always associated with some ethical positions. For that reason, supporters on both sides accuse each other of committing a specific 'cardinal sin' and we can see examples of this in the press every day. The left is commonly accused of being envious of those who have more and of having a tendency to destroy what it does not own or control. On the other hand, right-wingers are accused of falling into selfishness and arrogance with those who have less, thus generating a divided and classist society (where a privileged few have almost everything) that is not necessarily based on meritocracy or equal opportunities.

In this scenario, it seems that the dominant idea of the left (equality) and the dominant idea of the right (freedom) compete with each other. As a result, we are faced with a situation in which the greater equality we enjoy, the less individual freedom we have. The reverse would also be true; the more freedom individuals have, the less social equality there will be. One of the most significant differences between left and right parties today is what percentage of freedom and equality are necessary to create a better society.

Interestingly, the idea behind the European Union as we know it today supports equality among its members. It has affected the freedom (or liberties) of each individual country since they are no longer in charge of their fiscal or immigration policies. When the UK voted in 2016 to leave the European Union, it was intending to take back the freedom that, in its view, was taken by the European Union and its (rather leftist) ideals of equality.

Polar opposites

The ideological spectrum that covers the division between left/right is enormous and therefore not very useful. At one extreme, we would have societies in which the primary goal is absolute equality. A good example of that would be the Khmer Rouge regime in Cambodia (1975–1979). In its attempt to create a classless society where all members are absolutely equal, it evacuated every city and sent the whole population to work in fields. Banks, schools, hospitals and factories were closed, and money was banned. People wore the same clothes, and marriages were made between men and women at random. Individual freedom was reduced to the minimum possible expression in order to obtain full equality. In the process of creating this perfectly egalitarian society, a third of the total population of the country was exterminated.

At the other extreme, we could mention *anarcho-capitalism*. This is a political and economic movement that affirms that society does not need a state. The members of a society can voluntarily regulate themselves in a free market where all services are private. The functions of the police and judicial courts would be replaced by private defence agencies and insurance companies. All of them would be, of course, freely chosen by individuals. The privatisation of the state would eliminate the monopoly of specific functions that today belong to sovereign political states. This, in turn, would increase the individual freedom of citizens who could choose how to invest or spend their money. This view opposes the idea of handing it over to the state in the form of taxes over which they have no control.

Lenin giving a speech at the Putilov factory (Isaac Brodsky, 1929).

The two previous examples are merely extremes of a vast spectrum that among many others includes: anarchists, Marxists, Maoists, Trotskyists, socialists, centrists, liberals, neo-liberals, libertarians, Christian democrats, fascists, religious fundamentalists, etc. On top of that, we could also refer to the splits and internal nuances that may exist in each of these positions. These examples merely show the complex dialectical reality in which we move and, therefore, our political views should not be reduced to a simple choice between 'left or right'.

In developed Western countries, some sectors of the population that traditionally voted for left-wing political parties, today also vote for right-wing ones. It does not matter if, in the past, they fought for equal pay, equal rights and equal access to education. An obvious example is that of the industrial working class in many countries, which previously guaranteed left-wing governments with their numerical majority. However, after increasing their purchasing power and improving their conditions, they welcome the market economy and consumer societies.

In other cases, after industrial reconversions, many workers have lost their status as employees with stable jobs and reasonable salaries. Some populist parties with their ideological mix of left and right politics have found fertile ground in this layer of society. This can explain the success of previously marginal parties that now have become real alternatives[10].

Let's also remember how movements that today are clearly considered to have been right-wing, such as fascism or Nazism, declared themselves to be 'socialists'. In fact, many of their policies were typical of left-wing parties, and they had wide support from the working-class. For example, they were concerned about issues such as unemployment or the number of immigrants (as in the case of Jews in post-World War I Germany).

The label *'progressive'*

It seems that among a wide group of people, traditional political militancy has been replaced by support for certain social

---

10. The emergence of parties with an ideology traditionally considered as extremist in France, Italy, Hungary, Spain, Sweden, etc. respond to this pattern.

movements that are not necessarily left-wing or right-wing. Yet, the left has cleverly appropriated many of them and claims exclusive use of the adjective 'progressive'. At closer examination we can see that there is no reason why a right-wing party cannot be as progressive (or more so) than one on the left. For example, the rights of the LGTBQA+ community can be ideologically defended both from the leftist position favouring equality between all individuals and the rightist position which defends individual freedoms. The same goes for veganism, feminism, the fight against racism or climate change.

To further complicate matters, movements associated with the political right, such as white supremacism, nationalism or climate change denial, have claims that could perfectly fit in the program of many left-wing parties, such as economic protectionism and state intervention in the economy. Just remember how the 'progressive' Adolf Hitler considered himself to be a socialist, a vegetarian and an animal lover.

In today's complex society, there are feminists who are also racists, homosexuals who support white supremacism, members of the communist party who are Catholic and vegan Muslims. Therefore, any attempt to reduce the current ideological heterogeneity to the dualism left/right is doomed to failure. Reality overflows these ideas and makes them outdated in a post-modern era or at least in a society in transition from modernity to post-modernity.

Philosophical origins of the distinction

If we want to see the intellectual roots of the left and right movements, we must necessarily mention the German philosopher Georg Wilhelm Friedrich Hegel (1770–1831), who in his philosophy of law made an apology for the exaltation of the Prussian state in which he lived. He considered that Prussia, as a state, was the most elevated and perfect form of rationality in the history of humankind. It was a fairly abstract idea but one that had a practical consequence too, especially in the lives of its citizens. For Hegel, the evolution of rationality culminated in his own philosophy. The physical manifestation of that superior rationality was the state of Prussia and that should be defended no matter what.

Many authors writing after Hegel accepted his idea that 'rationality' manifested itself in the state. Depending on how one understands the role of this state, there are two resulting views: Right-wing Hegelians and left-wing Hegelians (of which Karl Marx is the most famous).

Jean-Jacques Rousseau (1712–1778) is also commonly mentioned as a reference for the left. In his opinion, inequality is artificial because in reality, human beings are born free and equal. We all are naturally good but society corrupts and separates us in many ways. But more on Rousseau later.

On the other hand, Friedrich Nietzsche (1844–1900), was famous for defending the exact opposite idea. He argued that equality between humans is purely artificial. In reality, we are all born unequal however society and religion strive to equalise us. Nietzsche thinks that this is unnatural because everyone has to artificially adapt to a 'morality of losers' that punishes the strong and the powerful but reward the weak or the mediocre.

These two contradictory views are at the basis of many political discussions between left and right. Being aware of that will not resolve any of the conflicts, but it will at least help to have greater intellectual clarity. Hopefully, this is enough to have a more rigorous and productive debate on the subject.

Conclusion

Today, left and right are very confusing terms that do not necessarily correspond to the political views of the individuals who claim to support them. The variability of possibilities is so great that saying that someone is left-wing or right-wing is almost an empty statement.

These two political ideas are often taken as decisive elements to make a moral judgment about a person. Judging someone by the colour of their vote in an election is an unacceptable reductionism. Individuals who vote for opposing parties may have much more in common than others who vote for the same party. Many of us, as members of post-modern societies, are politically fluid, at least as fluid as our circumstances allow. Originally, the distinction between left and right made sense, but today that difference has been blurred.

The manifestos of political parties in democratic countries are often very similar. They all seek to achieve a fairer and freer society. That is why sometimes the differences between parties are magnified to give voters the feeling that they are actually offering a real alternative. In Europe, today, many right-wing parties have similar goals to left-wing parties. The differences are in the details since almost all of them want to preserve the welfare state of social-democracies within a market economy.

One of the challenges of today is to focus on effectively overcoming the division between left and right. We are living the consequences of not doing so and we are having to experience an artificial and counterproductive ideological divide that has the media and social media as ideological battlefields without clear rules.

CHAPTER 5

THE ART OF CONFUSION

*'The reader's birth must occur
at the cost of the author's death.'*
(Roland Barthes)

Discussion

*Art means different things to different people, but what is art,
anyway? Do we all understand the same thing when we talk
about art? What are its defining characteristics? Are there rules
in art? Why do most people react so strongly against post-modern
art? Why do we feel so at odds when we enter a contemporary art
museum? Is contemporary art in complete decline or is it our idea
of art that is agonising? Is there any meaning in art?*

Introduction

Under the premise that *'everything that leaves the body must return to the body'*, the Spanish artist Paco Cao (1965) shocked the entire audience gathered that afternoon to participate in his performance. It was in fact a date to remember.

It was 1993 in Oviedo (Spain), in a small room on Paraíso Street. The artist announced that he had observed a strict diet based mainly on fabada (bean stew) during the previous days. His resulting excrement was bottled inside some glass jars that he showed to an already aghast audience. He asked attendees to please stay in the room (they didn't), and if anyone felt the need to throw up, they should do so on him, if they would be so kind.

By the time the jars were opened, the stench was already unbearable. When the artist began using its contents as a face cream and shampoo, many decided to leave. Paco Cao himself suffered seizures the moment he started using it as toothpaste.

That was probably his most controversial project, but without a doubt the most famous of all was when he decided to rent his body in the same way a car is leased. Choosing between three different rates, the client could hire his body exclusively (not including any type of conversation) or opt for an intermediate rate and limited human interaction. The full service, and therefore the most expensive ($135 per hour at the time), gave access to conversations of greater intellectual depth. Treating a living, human body as a commodity, the artist could create peculiar situations, for example regarding taxes, or customs fees if the clients were international. It was an original and curious way of treating the human body as a mere product. The project attracted a lot of international attention and later formed the content of a book which detailed some of the commissions he received.

Among the works he undertook was the remarkable occasion on which his body was hired in Germany for an exhibition in which he appeared naked, hands tied by a rope and hanging from the ceiling. On another occasion, he was hired to sit in a New York subway train for hours with his eyes closed, wearing a sign that read:

'This body has been rented to stay in this place for three hours. Please don't talk to this body or disturb it. If you have any suggestions, you can write them on the paper below. Thanks.'

The book details several of the jobs his body was hired for, such as when he was crucified in the United States by a church that needed someone to play Jesus Christ in a special mass. But, sure enough, one of the most peculiar was when a woman named María Gonzales, hired the body of the artist to accompany her through the streets of Manhattan as she insulted and humiliated him in public. The anecdotes are many, and his project aroused quite a good deal of curiosity. Paco Cao was interviewed on a prime-time show on Spanish television, and *The New York Times* wrote an article about him in 1996 titled 'But is He Art?'

What is art?

The question asked by the journalist from *The New York Times* was pertinent and not merely rhetorical. Can a body be considered art? Furthermore, can we really consider this type of conceptual art as art at all?

These are tough questions to answer if we consider them carefully. It is necessary to suppress the instinct to dismiss his performances as something stupid or an attempt to attract attention. In order to better understand Paco Cao's work and the evolution of art it is necessary to take a brief historical detour and see how art was understood in a modern world and how it has changed with the emergence of post-modernism. Listed below are four attempts to answer one of the most difficult questions in our time: 'What is art?'

Leonardo da Vinci sought in art the adequacy with reality.
Study of Horse (1488)

1. Imitation. If we understand art in a narrow sense, it would be nothing more than a simple imitation, a copy as perfect as possible of reality. Under this perspective art is seen as a mirror of nature. Plato considered that artists were im-

itators, simple artisans trying to replicate something that was more perfect. In fact, Plato did not have a good impression of artists because in his opinion, they were only degrading material things, and material things were already a degradation of ideas. In a hierarchy of importance, ideas (seen as the perfect reality) would come first, then material things (imperfect reality) and then art (copies of imperfect things). For Plato, art was the lowest level of reality. Unlike Plato, Leonardo da Vinci had a more positive image of artists, which is not surprising considering he was one himself. However, he also believed that the most perfect art was that closest to real life. He attached great importance to proportions and perspective in order to get as close to reality as possible.

2. Beauty. Others have understood art as something connected to beauty. The function of Art would be to produce beautiful things to the delight of the person who contemplates the work. It is irrelevant if there is an exact resemblance to reality or not. The goal is to produce an aesthetic pleasure, a pleasant reaction in the observer. A good work of art will have a soothing effect on the person who beholds it. The criterion for distinguishing good art from bad art is not its resemblance to reality but the pleasure that its intrinsic beauty produces in the spectator.

3. Creation. Another very different conception is that of art as the creation of forms or as a simple construction of things (for example a cathedral or a jewel). There is an identification between the artist and the craftsman who expertly creates objects by hand. Many of the objects that we find in history museums fit this type of vision. An expertly carved

tribal mask is considered an artistic object worthy of being displayed in a museum, even though we know nothing of its creator. In this case, we are not talking about an artist but a craftsman that produces 'artistic' and beautiful works.

4. Reconstruction. Anyone who visits a museum of contemporary art today knows that none of the previous definitions of art are appropriate to accommodate what we call 'contemporary art' (or post-modern art). A more inclusive definition is needed. Art is not something spiritual that comes from divine inspiration (or from the visit of the muses). Art needs to be understood as a reconstruction of something that is already given to us in the senses. This reconstruction is made by techniques that can be transmitted and repeated. This is how different traditions, styles and schools are created (Renaissance art, Dutch painting, Cubism, Expressionism, etc). Art is therefore the material manifestation of the ideas of a group or a society. It is not merely an act of individualism, no matter how much originality we want to attribute to the artist because according to this view, the environment will always condition their creations.

To have a clearer idea of what we call art, it is also necessary to distinguish between different types of art. On the one hand, we have the *fine arts* that are traditionally associated with painting, sculpture, architecture, music, poetry, theatre and dance. On the other hand, we have the so-called *decorative arts*, which have a practical function, in addition to an aesthetic value: ceramics, jewellery, cabinet making, fashion, etc.

This distinction arose in the Western cultural tradition. Consequently, such a difference did not exist in Oriental, African or pre-Columbian cultures. Some authors dated this distinction to the Renaissance and others somewhat later in the eighteenth century. The important thing here is that it was a functional and appropriate classification for a modern world but unfortunately is no longer appropriate today, in a time of transition between modernity to post-modernity. The technological and social development of our society has generated new forms of art that are difficult to frame if we consider the previous division (fine vs decorative). It is enough to think about photography, cinema, electronic music, graffiti, video games, performances, experimental cuisine, musicals, etc. Today, some of these creations are considered to be art, but not if we continue with the 'fine arts' mentality of the past. They simply do not fit in this category.

Four essential characteristics of art

To give a more inclusive definition of art that applies to both classical and contemporary art, the following aspects should be considered: the materials used, the agent of the work (artist), the intentionality (ideas, manifestos, etc.) and its spatiality (museum, church, etc.).

Let us not forget that the goal here is to reconcile ourselves with post-modern art and understand how it has changed. To be successful in this endeavour, it is mandatory to reconsider the characteristics that define art. In doing so, classical, modern and post-modern art will be included in that definition. Some basic characteristics of all art at any period of time are:

1. Materiality. Although there is a constant emergence of new techniques, new media, new schools and new trends; art requires a material support. There is no such thing as purely

spiritual art. Even in the most conceptual and avant-garde art, there is something material (a voice, a light, an empty room, a sound, a few words, a gesture, etc.).

2. Humanity. All art must be created by human beings (whether Neanderthal or *homo sapiens*). This assumes that there is no art produced by animals, gods or extra-terrestrials. This is not to say that we cannot appreciate pleasing aesthetic qualities in the drawings of a chimpanzee or beauty in a flower and the footprints left by a dinosaur thousands of years ago. Obviously, in a post-modern society there are new techniques that give the impression that the humans are not involved in the creation of art, for instance, artificial intelligence. However, these programmes are created and operated by humans and are instructed to create a painting, music, a sculpture or a poem.

3. Intentionality. Art is created by individuals with the intention of producing a work for the members of a social group. This implies that there is no 'universal art'. Any form of art is immersed in a tradition that determines the kind of art that is produced. Statements like 'music is a universal art' might sound very deep and meaningful but actually they are void of content. It would be more accurate to say that all known cultures produce music; but that does not mean that we can consider it as a work of art. It is like saying that 'speaking' is a universal language. All humans communicate through language but it is always a specific one: Spanish, English, Latin or Yoruba. Art (like a language) is something learned and transmitted whether academically or informally, as in the case of self-taught artists, but all of them are always steeped in tradition.

But is it art?

4. Spatiality. This aspect is directly connected with its materiality. The work of art needs a space within which to be
exhibited or represented. Traditionally, works of art, such
as paintings or sculptures, were confined to palaces, castles,
churches or cathedrals. Those were spaces connected with
political, religious or economic power. As we transitioned
through the modern world, the spaces became more public
and open to a larger section of society: museums, theatres,
auditoriums, etc. These places are built to spatially contain
works of art and are not necessarily centres of political or
religious power. For example, a cathedral contained within
itself the presence of God; therefore, everything inside that
cathedral acquired a sacred character just by being there,
in the presence of God. Museums, auditoriums and other
artistic spaces would be the secular version of the cathedral.

Everything they contain within them acquires the property of being 'art'. Like King Midas, they convert everything they touch into art. In other words, a certain painting is considered art because it is exhibited in a museum, and a musical composition is also art because it is performed in an auditorium with an audience. Irrespective of the quality of the music produced, a pop singer is considered an artist just by making music for 20 thousand people in an auditorium. However, a talented amateur pianist who plays for pleasure in their living room is not considered as such. The obvious conclusion here is that the space matters. The venue where a work is developed or exhibited is of great importance when calling it 'a work of art'. There is a clear social element in our consideration of art. As we have seen before, post-modernism is linked to individualism and some forms of art are not necessarily in public spaces but on private screens: phones, televisions, computers, etc.

The Birth of Venus (Botticelli, 1485).

The 'traditional' and the 'post-modern' version

As a mental experiment, just imagine the following for a few seconds: you enter a tall, Gothic cathedral. The light does not come from high windows with polychrome glass but from a disco-ball. The music you hear does not come from an organ but from a state-of-the-art sound system and, instead of a Requiem, loud electronic music is playing. The pictures on the walls are not the traditional Biblical scenes painted in classic style but graffiti of Jesus Christ, the Virgin Mary and the angels. From a traditional point of view, you may think that the sacred space has been desecrated.

Now, imagine that you enter an art museum. The exterior is a traditional building, all the workers are well-dressed and professional, the lighting is good and the interior is clean, spacious and neutral. The brochures are informative, and the guides organising the tours are experts in their field. However, instead of finding a painting by Botticelli, you find yourself in a room where a chair from Ikea is hanging by a thread and a light bulb turns on and off every 20 seconds. What would be the reaction of a visitor who has a rather traditional perception of art? They may say, 'This is nonsense', 'Is this art?', 'Bah, anyone can do that', or 'I just don't get it!'

Most probably, they would not be asking the same question if, instead of a chair, they were to find *The Birth of Venus*. However, it is doubtful that most people, on seeing this particular painting by Botticelli, would understand why this piece is widely considered to be a major work of art and what meaning it carries. In fact, who could explain what is meant by the figure of a naked woman with knee-length hair, perched on the shell of a giant scallop? Why is there a half-naked couple flying to her left? Who is the other woman on the right trying to cover her with a cape? The painting will make sense only for those who know about classic mythology, but few have that knowledge.

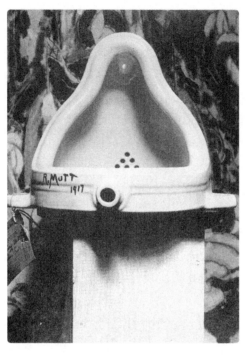

Readymade installations shifted the focus from the object to the place where the object is exhibited. Fountain (Marcel Duchamp, 1917).

In this state of affairs, there is a question we need to answer: why is a Botticelli painting considered art, but Paco Cao's performances are vehemently questioned?

For its part, post-modern art breaks with the need for technical difficulty, although it is fair to say that many contemporary works of art remain extraordinarily complicated. If being technically difficult to create is the criterion, art could be reduced to a mere craftsmanship. But art is more than that because, it is the material representation of an idea (or ideas) for a particular group of people. Art is aimed at a specific audience that is sometimes very large, and in some other occasions is just a tiny minority. Some of Botticelli's paintings were aimed at a very reduced group of people from a certain economic and cultural level, initially it was not produced to be contemplated by masses of tourists visiting a building that charges an entry fee.

Can graffiti be considered art? Portrait of singer Tino Casal in Tudela Veguín, Spain (Javier Robledo, 2018).

Post-modern artists, trying to move away and distance themselves from the traditional conception of art, have removed their works from their exclusive venues: museums, galleries, showrooms, auditoriums, etc. Today contemporary art is sprayed on trains, on city walls or in abandoned factories. There are landscape-artists that change the colour of the water in a river. There are performances that are held in bars, shopping centres or in the streets of a small town. The space for art is now more public.

Post-modern art, once it has been liberated from its material, spatial and technical limitations, then becomes more accessible to artists (although not always to viewers). It is no longer necessary to have an expensive workshop for painting or spend years learning complicated musical scales. There is no need to please a patron who pays for the artwork and the artists are not willing to make sacrifices or compromise in their creations. In very recent years it is interesting to observe how non-fungible tokens (unique digital identifiers that cannot be copied, substituted, or subdivided, that is recorded in a blockchain, and that is used to certify authenticity and ownership NFTs) and virtual art are increasingly distancing themselves from the traditional way of understanding art and how the art market works.

On the other hand, we cannot ignore the fact that in contemporary society, the number of works of art is far greater than the audience itself. The market is saturated with artists, and therefore they have to look for alternative ways of making their creations known. Sometimes, they seek to attract attention with something that they know will be provocative. This is not something new, this quest for impact among artists has been happening for centuries as they have had to compete for the attention of potential clients and also impress patrons. The purely commercial aspect of art tends to be ignored, but it has great relevance if we are to understand certain works of art in a capitalist society. Some pieces are created simply to attract attention in the same way that some digital media need click-baits. Artists try to stand out among the many others with whom they have to compete in exhibitions and in art fairs. It also happens in the fashion industry; the most extravagant models catch the attention, but the clothes in the stores are more conservative if they want to be economically viable.

Meaning in art

But what about the meaning of the artwork by Paco Cao? What idea did he want to represent when he smeared himself with his own excrement?

An external explanation to art itself would be that during the cold war the concept of art in the capitalist countries was reacting against the concept of art in the Soviet Union and its allies. Soviet art was more focused on cold rationalism, populist realism, and propaganda. In the West, and as a reaction to this restrictive artistic imposition, a more irrational and more emotional abstract art started to develop. Paco Cao is part of this less restrictive and open tradition where art can also be a form of protest or an irreverent act.

A less sociological explanation suggests that the message that Paco Cao wants to convey is his self-assertion in the need for a new type of art. There is an attempt to break with the traditional conception of art. His performance was free from spatial limitations because it took place in a simple room, not in a museum. He introduced new materials as he used his own excrement, not traditional paints. There was a different conception of the audience; the attendants interacted actively in the performance and they were an integral part of it. There was no compliance with the idea of beauty as the goal of art. For Paco Cao, ugliness, disgust and physical pain can also be art. The duration of the artwork was also different as the performance lasted only a few minutes. This is nothing compared to the centuries of some paintings or the millennia of classical sculptures. However, the impression on the spectators probably lasted a long time.

In contemporary art, there is a tendency to consider the idea (or the theory) as something more important than the material artwork itself. This is commonly described as 'conceptual art'. Knowing beforehand the idea behind the artwork prepares the public to see everything under a different light as they know what to expect. 'Everything that leaves the body must return to the body' sums up the idea represented by Paco Cao quite well, and once we are aware of what he wanted to represent, the performance is more easily interpretable.

It is also true that much of the artwork in contemporary art is influenced by post-modern art theory. In a lecture titled, 'Post-modernism Revisited', Frederic Jameson writes the following regarding post-modern art:

(...) critics and theoreticians of all kinds assure us that our situation is that of the end of art as an object, that of its volatilization, that of its transformation into something else. The prosperity of the art market, the rise of an ever-increasing number of galleries and auction houses, the very transformation of the traditional lethargic museum into a noisy and popular social and cultural meeting place, all these are, without a doubt, clear testimony of that something like art is still very much alive, even if it has been turned into merchandise everywhere.

Jameson also points out that post-modern art (the art that in his opinion characterizes today's neoliberal capitalist societies) dispenses with styles and schools unlike modern art:

The previous art, what we call modern or modernism, was described by Roland Barthes and others as the invention of a style, the search for a personal and unique style, in such a way that it distinguished each modern artist from the others and this was also true for literature, for music, for painting and for the cinema.

In this sense, post-modern art no longer recognises the concept or ideal of a style.

This theory denies the possibility of having a single or dominant interpretation of any artwork. It even denies that the artist's interpretation is more relevant or has more value than any other interpretation. The French philosopher Roland Barthes (1915–1980) described this phenomenon as 'the death of the author'. Authors are free to say whatever they want about their own work, but the reader/observer/listener will instead understand what they can, and that is the relevant meaning.

There is no single meaning for Paco Cao's performance. Each attendee has their own interpretation, and it will often be different from that of the author himself. The meaning of his work is not univocal, instead its meaning is disseminated. None of those interpretations is the dominant one. In fact, in a post-modern society there should be no dominant interpretation because that would be authoritarian, undemocratic and repressive.

There is an essential change in the way art is perceived in post-modernity. Previously, art was seen as something very serious and profound; something closer to a religion. Art was something to be contemplated and observed from a certain ontological distance, it was an almost divine production from a creative artist (a demiurge, in Platonic terminology). In contrast, post-modernism removes this serious and arrogant character from art and introduces an element of playfulness. It seems as if post-modernism wants to give a wake-up call to artists, critics, curators, spectators and other actors in the artistic field, crying, 'Don't take it so seriously, it's just art!'. There is no deep meaning, in fact there is no meaning at all.

Instead *the author is dead* and there are innumerable meanings, all of them valid.

Conclusion

If we accept the propositions of contemporary art, we can reconcile ourselves with the Ikea chair hanging from a thread as being a legitimate work of art. On the other hand, if we insist on maintaining the traditional and narrow perception of art, it is only a chair hanging from a thread in a space that should be occupied by proper artwork, such as Botticelli's *The Birth of Venus.*

We cannot forget either that art is influenced by the type of society in which it exists. Art can no longer be as it was in previous eras when a work of art was produced for an aristocratic class or for the Church. Today, many of the artists have other jobs and do not necessarily need to make a living from what they sell. This is the reason why they can allow themselves to be more experimental or transgressive with the rules without affecting their living conditions too much.

Everything that has been said so far, however, does not mean that all contemporary art is good. There is bad art in the same way that there are bad artists. If a group of people with very limited musical knowledge forms a band and play three chord songs we would not question if what they are producing is music or not. However, depending on our tastes and education we will deem that music interesting or not, and something very similar happens with art. What distinguishes a good artwork from a bad one is something even more complex and open to debate.

CHAPTER 6

THE HUMAN ANIMAL

'If anybody said that I should die
if I did not take beef tea or mutton,
even on medical advice,
I would prefer death.
That is the basis of my vegetarianism.'

(Mahatma Gandhi)

Discussion

The perception of the human being in post-modern philosophy is something new. Our ideas of humans and animals have changed throughout history. Today, we are debating whether we should extend some of our rights to animals or not. If so, can we also expect some duties from them? We are adopting 'new' eating habits that do not include proteins of animal origin and are questioning whether it is morally acceptable to use furs in which to clothe ourselves. More controversially, can we use animals for medical experimentation? Are humans essentially different from other animals? Are all animal species equal? Is speciesism a form of discrimination like racism or sexism?

Introduction

The reproductive capacity of some species of rabbits is such that, under optimal conditions, about 30 million descendants can emerge from a single pair in the short span of three years. It is an exponential increase that would put the balance of any ecosystem at risk.

For Australia, a continent that had evolved independently over millions of years and developed some peculiar ecological characteristics, this would inevitably become a problem. In fact, it was more than that, it was a complete disaster.

It all started innocently enough when, in 1859, Thomas Austin imported European rabbits for his Victorian estate in South Australia. He wanted to let them run free and breed so that he could later do some hunting. Besides, it was not the first time that rabbits had been brought to Australia. The reality is that no one, at that point, could ever imagine the catastrophe that was coming.

Thomas Austin was a member of the Acclimatisation Society, a volunteer organisation that became especially popular during the nineteenth and early twentieth centuries, coinciding with the European colonial period. The idea was to introduce new species of animals and plants into the newly colonised territories. In turn, they introduced in Europe species that were considered exotic, had medicinal value or were useful for other practical purposes. The large population of European eucalyptus trees, for example, come from Australia. They were a species of tree that grew rapidly and were therefore useful in the reforestation of large, previously deforested territories.

The ultimate goal of the acclimatisation societies was to enrich the flora and fauna of all countries. It was a very noble objective. However, what the members of these societies failed to understand at the time was that species live in a permanent struggle for resources, and the introduction of a new species is often made at the expense of another. Today, eucalyptus trees are considered an invasive species in some areas since they compete and destroy other native species. In all fairness, it must be said that it was a time when the theories of Charles Darwin were not yet very well known, and ecology had not been developed as a scientific discipline. It is easier for us to see in hindsight the mistake it was in the long term.

Thomas Austin in 1888.

Many of the British settlers tried to introduce new species of plants and animals to 'correct' the supposed natural deficiency of some of the colonies within the British empire. These settlers were clearly nostalgic for their homelands and they tried to recreate the landscape by introducing species from the British Isles.

Thomas Austin was just one of those settlers who also had a passion for hunting. When he arrived in Australia, he wanted to continue that practice. He wrote to his nephew asking him for 12 grey rabbits. Unable to get that number, his nephew decided to send specimens of another breed as well. In turn, these two breeds interbred to form a third one that was particularly well adapted to Australian conditions.

In less than 10 years, the situation was already out of control. In 50 years, rabbits had spread over an area greater than half of Europe. It is the largest increase in the number of mammals ever recorded in history (at least on one particular continent). The rabbits wiped out the vegetation of large areas and were responsible for a serious problem: deforestation. Vast areas that were previously grassy were reduced to desert.

In 1887, the government of New South Wales offered $25,000[11] to anyone who could find an effective method of eradicating the problem. However, out of nearly 1,500 suggestions, none could be found that was both effective and safe for humans and other species of animals.

Due to the extreme seriousness of the problem, the government could not stand idly by. It was imperative to do something to reverse the situation. As of that moment, farmers were free to eliminate as many rabbits as possible. Unfortunately, this measure was far from sufficient to reduce their number so they decided that they would erect barrier fences to prevent rabbits from advancing further. In addition to that, all access to water sources was covered so they would die of thirst during heat waves. But all seemed futile. In the 1950s, the situation was so worrying that the government decided to introduce a new strategy: biocontrol. Several rabbits infected with the

---

11. More than $1,000,000 in today's money.

myxomatosis virus (which only affects rabbits) were released. At first, the measure seemed to be effective and both farmers and the authorities were optimistic for the first time.

Rabbit skins in Australia were abundant (c.1905).

The population of 600 million was reduced to about 100 million, but the rabbits developed immunity against the virus, and the population began to recover. By the 1990s, given the persistence of the problem, another pathogen was introduced: the rabbit haemorrhagic disease virus (known as RHDV). In combination with the poison that was being used, there was a significant reduction in the number of rabbits. However, even today, the problem persists, and experts continue to search for solutions to reduce the number further. The fly that transmits the RHDV virus cannot survive in colder areas and rabbits retreat there, where the populations are still too large.

Speciesism

It is practically impossible to determine the total number of rabbits that have been eliminated by these methods but it could be in the hundreds of millions. In situations like this, some organisations for the defence of animals use terms such as 'holocaust'. In their opinion, it is not an exaggeration to use this word since, according to the dictionary, it refers to organised, systematic killings by a state. Many others consider it a misuse of the term when it is referred to rabbits. Furthermore, they even deny the possibility of applying the term "holocaust" to any species other than humans. This, in turn, creates controversy because some groups in favour of animal liberation believe that this is a clear case of discrimination. They also have a name for this practice: speciesism.

The term 'speciesism' means treating animals differently from how we treat the humans. We view them (animals in general) differently simply because they belong to another species. Humans have a tendency to treat animals from a position of superiority. For the advocates of animal rights this is intolerable. They are ready to fight discrimination between species in the same way that today we fight against racism or sexual discrimination. They argue that we even should stop using the word 'animals' to distinguish them from us because humans are also animals, and there is nothing that makes us special.

As a result of this theory, all species are considered entirely equal, including the human animal. None is above the other, and we have no reason to feel superior or treat other species as inferior. If we agree that slavery is morally wrong, then forcing animals to work or killing them for food is equally wrong.

Some academics are deeply committed to the defence of animal rights, such as the famous Australian philosopher Peter Singer (1946). In his popular book *Animal Liberation,* he controversially argues that many humans have lower intelligence than some non-human animals. It is for this reason that the argument of human intellectual superiority is not valid. Humans with intellectual disabilities, babies or patients who have suffered brain injuries have fundamental rights, which such animal rights defenders believe, we deny to animals with higher levels of intelligence (for example, chimpanzees or orang-utans).

Singer's main argument is that animals have the capacity to feel pain and suffer, and for him this is the deciding factor that makes us equal. It is not necessary to be an ethologist who studies animal behaviour to acknowledge that animals also feel pain. Therefore, it is argued, it is morally unacceptable to cause them suffering if we can avoid it. In an article called 'All animals are equals' he argues:

A *liberation movement demands an expansion of our moral horizons and an extension or reinterpretation of the basic moral principle of equality. Practices that were previously regarded as natural and inevitable come to be seen as the result of an unjustifiable prejudice. Who can say with confidence that all his or her attitudes and practices are beyond criticism? If we wish to avoid being numbered amongst the oppressors, we must be prepared to re-think even our most fundamental attitudes. We need to consider them from the point of view of those most disadvantaged by our attitudes, and the practices that follow from these attitudes. If we can make this unaccustomed mental switch we may discover a pattern in our attitudes and practices that consistently operates so as to benefit one group—usually the one to which we ourselves belong—at the expense of another. In this way we may come to see that there is a case for a new liberation movement. My aim is to advocate that we make this mental switch in respect of our attitudes and practices towards a very large group of beings: members of species other than our own—or, as we popularly though misleadingly call them, animals. In other words, I am urging that we extend to other species the basic principle of equality that most of us recognize should be extended to all members of our own species.*

Singer and his followers propose adopting a vegan diet (or at least vegetarian). They advocate for the prohibition of animal experimentation in laboratories and their use in shows, zoos or farms. They believe some species, like donkeys, horses and dogs, are being used as slaves and need to be liberated. In short, they have a clear ethical stance: to eliminate any practice that causes pain to animals and is not oriented to the promotion of their welfare.

'The most dangerous man in the world' and The Great Ape Project

Peter Singer was the person who in 1993 launched the Great Ape Project. With substantial international support, the project posed the following question: if other hominids, such as Neanderthals, had not become extinct and were living among us today, would we hesitate to grant them the same rights as ourselves? Would we treat them differently? If the answer is 'no', then why not also grant those rights to chimpanzees, bonobos, gorillas and orang-utans?

Among other things, the Great Ape Project calls for three basic rights for all species: the right to life, the right to freedom and the prohibition of torture. Their motto, *equality beyond humanity*, is a clear example of how we should over-come speciesism.

Peter Singer's views have been influential beyond the con-fines of academia, being a well-known figure internationally. However, he has as many detractors as followers. Some of his critics accuse him of being 'the most dangerous man in the world'. In fact, his ideas are quite radical even for some of his defenders. In an attempt to be consistent with his doctrines, he admits that if there is equality between species, sexual re-lations between humans and other species of animals would be justified in certain specific circumstances (only when it is mutually satisfying).

His views on infanticide are also extremely controversial since in his opinion, there would be no problem in allowing the killing of babies in the first moments of life.

Although Peter Singer himself despises the image of 'the most dangerous man in the world', the truth is that his ideas lie quite far from general opinion and that they contrast with the gentle image of Singer himself.

The reality, however, is that a milder version of his ideas has a considerable influence in our society and his arguments are picked up by many groups in favour of animal rights every-where. With great satisfaction, these groups have witnessed in recent years the rising popularity of diets that do not include animal products. Even companies like McDonald's now offer a menu suitable for vegans.

Vegetarians, vegans and 'ahimsa'

Vegetarianism is not, by any account, a novel practice. Evi-dence shows that 4,000 years ago, it was already common in some parts of India.

A central element for the development of vegetarianism is the concept of 'ahimsa'. This is a principle of non-violence that applies to any living being and is present in several Asian religions, such as Buddhism, Hinduism and Sikhism. In the West, it was made popular by the teachings of Mahatma Gandhi and his non-violent resistance movement. Later, Gandhi had a great influence on various movements that peacefully campaigned for the civil rights of certain groups. Probably the best-known of them all was the civil-rights movement for African Americans led by Martin Luther King Jr.

Behind the practice of vegetarianism is the belief that killing or harming any living being is morally reprehensible. Every living being participates in the same divine element and, therefore, if we harm them, we are harming ourselves. According to the law of karma, if we do something bad, like killing a living creature, at some point, something bad will happen to us. The American anthropologist, Marvin called this type of religious explanation given by the people involved in the practice, *emic*. However, he thought that there is always a scientific and rational explanation, termed *etic*, that is connected to the material conditions of life[12]. When trying to explain why Hindus do not eat cows despite being surrounded by thousands of them or why Muslims avoid eating pork meat, he writes:

To explain different patterns of culture we have to begin by assuming that human life is not merely random or capricious. (...) Another reason why many customs and institutions seem so myste-

---

12. *Emic* explanation is the study of cultural norms that are specific to one group of people or within one culture. Internal.
    Etic involves the analysis of cultural phenomena from the perspective of one who does not participate in the culture. External.

rious is that we have been taught to value elaborate 'spiritualised' explanations of cultural phenomena [emic] more than down-to-earth material ones [etic]. (...) even the most bizarre-seeming beliefs and practices turn out on closer inspection to be based on ordinary, banal, one might say 'vulgar' condition, needs and activities. What I mean by banal or vulgar solution is that rests on the ground and that it is built up out of guts, sex, energy, wind, rain, and other palpable and ordinary phenomena.

The idea is that there is a material and, almost always, unconscious material justification that explains practices such as vegetarianism, veganism or the rejection of beef and pork. Instead, the explanation given by its practitioners is religious, spiritual or metaphysical and therefore much more difficult to contradict.

Vegetarianism was not a relevant movement in the West until the nineteenth century, when it began to be practised in small communities of England and the United States. These groups were influenced by Hinduism at a time when colonialism brought Eastern religions closer to the West. As a consequence, some of their members adopted vegetarianism in their daily lives. Within these groups, there were individuals who took this doctrine to the extreme and only consumed products that did not come from animals. They eliminated eggs and dairy from their diet, but they still had not coined the word 'vegan'.

It was in 1944 when a scion of the British Vegetarian Society created a publication called *Vegan News*. The word 'vegan' was formed from the first and last letters of the word 'vegetarian' (veg + an = vegan). Although other names were proposed for this practice, this was the one that ultimately prevailed. Among other goals, with the word "vegan", they were trying to symbolise the beginning and the end of vegetarianism.

Hunting scene in the 14th century.

Today, the aim of many animal rights activists is to turn carnivores and vegetarians into vegans. For this, they not only use ideological or moral arguments (such as that of ahimsa) but resort to arguments that they know may be more effective in a post-modern society. They highlight the virtues of the vegan diet for health and aesthetic reasons. Today, veganism is not just an ideology but a social practice and, sometimes, a powerful marketing tool as we see in the 'healthy' products of today and its gurus that advocate to abstain from eating meat. In their words, that Veganism will make us better, not only morally but also physically and aesthetically.

Nature vs Walt Disney

Those who disagree with this approach and oppose the fight for equality between species, have a totally different vision of nature (in general) and animals (in particular). For them, nature is neither harmonious nor kind. Animals are in a constant struggle and some species attack and eat others. The example of rabbits in Australia is just one of the thousands that we could find to prove the dialectical relationship among species. Even between members of the same species the conflict is permanent over basic needs such as food, territory or mating. This results in violent fights that can wipe out entire groups. It is well documented that even among those that are most similar to us, such as chimpanzees, there are planned attacks on rival clans. If a group has to be eliminated, there is no distinction between males, females or infants. In fact, it is very likely that Neanderthals became extinct because of their direct competition with *h*. Our species eliminated the competition, and it is likely that the same thing happened with many other species in the evolutionary history of modern humans.

Anti-speciesists have been widely criticised for having a highly idealised image of nature, and that includes animals and their ecosystems. They are said to have a somewhat childish view of 'nature' not far removed from Walt Disney movies. When we see two cute squirrels playing in the park, what they are actually doing is fighting aggressively for their right to use a certain space. When we hear the song of a bird in the morning, it is not a sweet melody of Mother Nature but the competition between individuals of the same species to attract a female or drive away rivals.

It is also important to note that the argument of animal suffering that Peter Singer invokes is not fully convincing for his detractors. In many cases, he is considering very different species and there is no way to measure degrees of suffering. Would the suffering of a fish be greater than that of a child deprived of the animal protein necessary for full physical and

intellectual development? In fact, it is proven that the inges-
tion of meat (together with the dominance of fire and the use
of weapons) made the brain of the human species to grow and
evolve to what it is today. Our brain capacity increased enormously thanks to the intake of animal protein. Consequently,
the level of intelligence in humans is much higher than those
of other primates. If pressured with the argument of vegetarianism, one could conclude that eating meat has made us human. We have not become extinct like other species similar to
ours thanks to our adaptive capacity. Therefore, eating meat
is not something that one has to justify but rather the opposite; if anything it is vegans and vegetarians who should justify
themselves for not doing so.

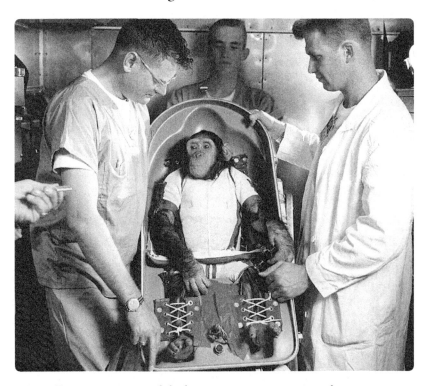

*Experimentation with higher primates is a controversial practice.
The chimpanzee Ham (pictured in 1963) was sent on a space trip
to observe the effects.*

Rights and duties

Species such as higher primates (chimpanzees, orang-utans, gorillas, gibbons and bonobos) have a higher level of intelligence than other species of animals, and, consequently, their ontological status[13] is also superior. Very few people would really argue that a chicken and a chimpanzee are on the same level. For us, protecting apes is almost an obligation, if only for a selfish reason. It is imperative that we study them since they share more than 99% of human genes (although a dog shares 75%). Understanding apes would help us understand ourselves as a biological species. Luckily, there is a wide consensus on the studying and protecting of big primates and there are numerous ecological reserves where they can live freely and without risk of harm from humans. However, if we equate all species and treat them the same, we could not be justified in protecting primates as we do at the moment. In that case, we would be explicitly admitting that they are more important than other species.

More problematic though, are the cases of captivity or scientific and pharmaceutical experimentation. In an attempt to provide an introduction to the issues raised by the use of primates in scientific research, the Medical Research Council (MRC) and the Wellcome Trust produced a booklet called 'Primates in Medical Research'. In it we can read the following:

Ideally, primates would not have to be used in medical research. They are used only when no satisfactory alternatives exist – in other words, when there is no other way to advance knowledge in an es-

---

13. Its relative importance to us in the hierarchy of things that exist in the world.

sential area of medical science, or to be as sure as possible that new treatments for serious diseases are safe to test on humans.

It goes on to state that the advances produced in medicine have been very important:

Many significant advances in modern medicine have been based on research involving primates, including the following:

- *Polio vaccines, which have virtually eliminated the disease in the USA and Europe since the 1950s.*
- *Life-support systems for premature babies.*
- *Kidney dialysis.*
- *Anti-rejection drugs for organ transplant recipients.*
- *Deep brain stimulation to suppress the symptoms of Parkinson's disease.*
- *Surgical treatment for macular degeneration – an incurable eye disease that is the primary cause of blindness in older people.*
- *New techniques in stroke rehabilitation therapy.*
- *Drugs to combat asthma.*

The debate is not at all easy, especially considering all those advances that could have not been achieved without primates.

Besides, we could not freely speak of 'equality among species' since that would mean extending the rights of humans to animals, and this is a different matter. The rights are given by states and do not appear in nature (because 'natural rights' do not exist). In most cases, rights are also accompanied by some duties, and that would not be possible to demand from animals. For example, the right to life is accompanied by the obligation not to kill, but animals cannot understand that. The idea of law is purely human and not transferable to animals. In today's contemporary societies, we accept rights without obligations, but only in certain exceptional cases (as with people with severe mental disabilities or people with reduced learning capacity). This is because of an ethical assumption that we all are humans. However, in the past such individuals were locked up or simply eliminated. In primitive societies, the elderly, the sick or new-borns were sacrificed or left to die when times of scarcity came. There was no ethical consideration beyond the preservation of the group. In post-modern societies, it does not seem acceptable because our material conditions are very different and the preservation of the individual is the norm. In most Western countries we have covered our basic needs and this is partly thanks to farming and raising animals for human consumption. Our moral values of today are very different. They have changed because our material conditions have also changed.

In earlier times there was no problem in presenting the animals as they were on the plates. Today many consider it in bad taste. The Allegory of Senses: Hearing, Touch, and Taste (detail), 1618, Jan Breughel the Elder.

Another problem that we would need to face if we were to accept the premise that all animals have the same rights as humans is that of 'justice'. What should we do with an animal that attacks a human being? What happens when one animal eliminates another member of its own species? Can they be measured with the same standards as humans are? Can we judge and punish them? Do we need animal tribunals? It all seems unlikely.

Animals and human animals

Historically, in the Western tradition, the ontological status of animals (their position in the hierarchy of existence) has changed enormously.

In the first phase of humanity (Stone Age), some animals were the object of veneration. There are many examples of cave paintings that were most likely also places of worship and adoration. Bison or wild horses were a source of food, but they were also feared as they could cause death or severe injuries. On many occasions, it was the animals that controlled the humans.

Later, as humans domesticated and tamed some animals, their divine status was lowered. The gods became anthropomorphic, as is evident in the religions of Greece and Rome (although still morphing to animals or monsters from time to time). By the time Christianity or Islam arrived, animals were fully subjugated to humans and were seen as mere machines. Even during the Middle Ages, and until the seventeenth century, animals were thought to have no souls, and that clearly distinguished them from human beings. However, after scientific advances in the study of animal genetics and animal psychology, it has been shown that the closeness between some primates and human beings is so great that it would be ridiculous to reduce them to machines that act only through stimuli.

After the development of Darwinism and ethology (the science studying animal behaviour) it has become clear that primates are living organisms capable of feeling basic emotions similar to ours.

Post-industrial societies have moved so far away from contact with their food that there is a feeling of estrangement with them. In countries like the UK, many restaurants serve fish without the head to avoid reminding diners that they are about to eat an animal that was alive until not long ago. Similarly, many people who like meat and have no problem consuming it, consider it cruel and unnecessary to serve dishes such as roast suckling pig with its head. It is something macabre that reminds them that the animal had to be sacrificed for them.

This distancing between humans and the animals that serve us as food is relatively recent and has generated a sensitivity that can be extreme. Now, our only contact with animals of a certain size are the pets we live with, and therefore we apply the same empathy with the animals we eat as with our dogs and cats.

Eating only vegetables does not make us morally better or necessarily healthier. There is no kind of superiority associated with rejecting foods of animal origin, especially if we consider that the cultivation of these vegetables can require enormous amounts of land, water and fertilisers that sometimes destroy the habitat of many animals.

Conclusion

It is impossible to live in the world without having an impact on it. There is no room for neutrality even if we insist on it. However, this does not invalidate the claim by animal rights advocates that living conditions on sweat farms are cruel and easy to improve. Moreover, the less extreme activists, claim that meat consumption should be reduced in some countries for being excessive. The rate of meat production as the world population increases becomes more difficult to sustain, except if we consider the animals as mere objects. If animals, especially those that serve us as food, become mere objects of consumption, and we find no connection with them, then we should worry.

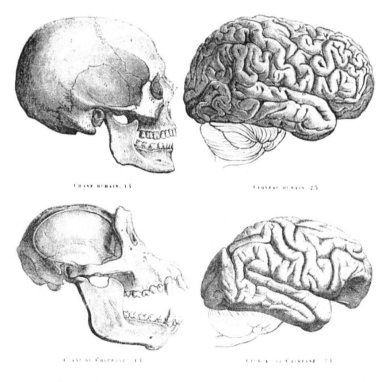

Differences between the human brain and that of a chimpanzee.

158

The situation today has generated new philosophical problems that did not exist before. Although the positions are sufficiently opposed, some kind of commitment could be reached. That would be a partial concession to some of the demands of animal rights defenders: On the one hand, the consumption of animal meat would not be eliminated, but in return, the conditions in which animals live and die would be improved.

If there is a consensus to reduce polluting gas emissions and transition to renewable energies, states could also introduce specific regulations to put an end to some practices. The goal is to improve the general welfare of animals. Even if it is only from a selfish perspective, the improvement in their conditions would affect the quality of our food and consequently be beneficial to our health.

The other great challenge would be to find the exact point of equilibrium so that the price of the food production does not increase too much and people with fewer resources are excluded. There is a risk that this might work only in richer countries, and these are problems for a new reality.

CHAPTER 7

CLIMATE OF CHANGE

'You have stolen my dreams
and my childhood.'
(Greta Thunberg)

Discussion

Who could possibly deny that there is a major climate change in the making? But, is it not always the case? Can we go so far as to say that there is a 'climate emergency' or a 'climate crisis'? Is human activity the only thing responsible for that change? Does this planet need to be 'saved'? And what do we understand by 'nature', anyway? What is our place in the world? Are we part of nature or are we something altogether different?

Introduction

According to one legend, Tutu Pele arrived on the island of Hawaii from Tahiti escaping from her sister Namaka. The incident started when she tried to seduce her brother-in-law. When her sister realised what was going on she flew into a rage and began to chase Tutu Pele with the intention of killing her. Tutu Pele was no angel at all and from a very young age she was known for her hot temper, violent reactions and complicated character. Her sister, Namaka, was convinced that Tutu Pele was capable of exterminating her own family if necessary. In order to stop her and all the damage she could cause, Namaka decided to end her sister's life.

Tutu Pele, also known as Madame Pele, is a jealous and capricious goddess, passionate and very powerful. She is the deity that controls the flow of lava on the island of Hawaii. Some of her siblings are the clouds, the waves, the wind, the rain and the fire. Namaka chased her sister through more than 4,000 kilometers until finally there was a confrontation between the two. Tutu Pelle came off worst and Namaka left her lying on the ground thinking that she was dead. However, Tutu Pele managed to recover and today she dwells in the volcanoes of the island.

In Hawaiian mythology she randomly appears to tourists, and some locals too, in order to warn them of an impending eruption. She is symbolically represented as a young woman in a red dress but sometimes she can also appear as an old woman with a white dog. In particular, Tutu Pele is identified with the Kilauea volcano because it is the most active on the entire island despite the fact that the neighbouring volcano (Mauna Loa) is much more imposing in size. This might partly explain why some inhabitants still believe that this volcano is the true home of Tutu Pele.

It is, paradoxically, in Mauna Loa (a place associated with destruction, magic and the irrational) where the scientists (using data, reason and logic) first raised their concerns about the rising temperatures. Initially, they gave the voice of alarm and subsequently showed the need to act decisively on what was later called climate change and global warming.

Mauna Loa is the largest and the second highest of the five volcanoes that make up the island of Hawaii. On its northern slope, 3,397 metres above sea level, is located the weather station where the measurement of CO_2 in the atmosphere has been recorded since 1958. Not only is this the world's oldest registry, it also provides the world reference in terms of gas emissions on the whole planet.

Mauna Loa was chosen as the place to make this type of measurement due to its remote location. Being far from any continent, it can provide a more accurate picture of air quality and the impact of CO_2 emissions on a planetary level. Pollution from other nearby volcanoes is taken into account and duly discounted. This allows the results to be calibrated so that the final figure is not affected.

For decades, the person responsible for these measurements was Charles Keeling (1928–2005), an American scientist who is credited for making popular a hypothesis that was controversial at the time but that today few people would question. The premise of this hypothesis is that human activity (especially industrial) causes an increase in greenhouse gases; however, the oceans cannot absorb CO_2 emissions as fast as it was initially thought and the temperature of the planet rises constantly every year. This, in combination with some other factors, has generated what is now known as the 'greenhouse effect'.

The infamous 'greenhouse effect' is a process by which four gases: water vapor, CO_2, methane and ozone prevent heat from leaving the atmosphere, consequently increasing the overall temperature of the planet. This hypothesis is not original to Charles Keeling but paraphrasing Isaac Newton, we could say that he stood on the shoulders of giants. It is also necessary to give credit to other scientists such as Svante Arrhenius (1859–1927) and the observations of the often-forgotten Eunice Foote (1819–1888), the American scientist who also fought for the defence of women's rights.

Mauna Loa Observatory (MLO) in Hawaii

With his constant measurements, it was Keeling who observed that there was a huge variation in the amounts of CO_2 each year depending on the season. During the beginning of spring in the Northern Hemisphere, the amounts of CO_2 in the atmosphere were reduced thanks to the ability of forests and plants to absorb this gas. However, the amounts rose again in autumn and winter, but always from a starting point higher than the previous year. This meant that annually the amount of CO_2 in the atmosphere was constantly increasing. That had a direct impact on the global temperature of the planet. The data collected by Keeling showed an upward curve in the amount of gas. Today, this phenomenon is known as the 'Keeling Curve'.

In July 1997, a few years before his death, the then Vice-President of the United States, Al Gore, awarded Keeling a well-deserved prize in recognition for his exceptional scientific contributions over 40 years.

A more conscious society

If we are talking about the perils of global warming today, it is thanks to Keeling's measurements and detailed observations. He was definitively responsible for increased awareness of the situation and he also helped politicians pay more attention to this worrying phenomenon. Thanks to his work, the data available could not be ignored anymore.

This concern regarding the changing pattern of the climate also reached the press in the 1980s, especially in the state of California. For the first time, journalists began to connect natural phenomena such as heatwaves, droughts or wildfires with global warming. Today, this is the norm, but at the time, it was something completely new. In fact, the risk in the present is to attribute to global warming any climatic phenomenon that is outside normal parameters. In other words, there are many phenomena that could be explained by 'natural causes', but the media and popular opinion will immediately attach them to global warming provoked by human activity. Even for expert scientists, it is difficult to draw a dividing line between the natural and human causes.

It is also very interesting to see how some people do not consider 'natural' what is caused by humans. This is, in itself, very relevant as we will see later in this chapter.

Already since the late 1960s, there was an environmental awareness in Western societies. *Greenpeace,* the campaigning network, was formed in Canada at the end of that decade. It was motivated by the protests against the nuclear tests that the President of the United States, Richard Nixon, carried out in Alaska. It was a time of considerable environmental pessimism and the predictions of some academics were not rosy either. Marine biologist Rachel Carson published a book called *Silent Spring* in which she criticised the use of chemical pesticides such as DDT for their harmful effect on the natural world. Another popular book published in 1968 was *The Population Bomb,* written by Paul and Anne Ehrlich. The book predicted a world famine in the 1970s and 80s due to the constant increase in population. Other concerns at the time were the depletion of oil reserves, the dependence on the automobile in modern life, the ecological impact of the Vietnam War and the effects of nuclear energy. Some groups were calling for a 'back to nature' lifestyle which, in practical terms, implied living a simpler life and consuming organic products that were locally cultivated by them. They were also very critical of mass consumption and, in step with the times, they advocated for a 'less is more' way of living.

All these concerns were present in the life of many people during the sixties and seventies, especially the younger generation that gathered for events like the student revolts in France, the 'summer of love' or the Woodstock festival.

Another important date for environmentalism was the 22nd of April 1970. It was the first time that Earth Day was celebrated, and it turned out to be a success of participation. There were demonstrations and protests in several countries and the organisers had as reference the protests against the Vietnam War and the Civil Rights movement in the United States. This meant that there was some kind of connection between these political claims and the environmental concern. Many of the people involved were linked to the hippie movements of the time and they were associated with a particular ideology. However, this does not mean that their concerns were not legitimate or that they should be dismissed as a caricature.

Today, many of those who demonstrate in the streets for a green legislation consider themselves to be continuing this fight against governments, companies, mass-production and the consumerism system. However, they cannot be condemned as hippies with loose ideals of counterculture and anti-establishment dreams. They are a much more heterogeneous movement that ranges from retirees to middle-class college students or devotee members of Christian churches.

Another major difference with the ecologist movement of the 1960s is today's idea of saving the planet by consuming. It is not about giving up anything and living in a simpler way, but about consuming differently: electric cars, sustainable fashion, meat alternatives, solar panels, recycled products, etc. In fact, many of these products are much more expensive than traditional ones, so not everyone has access to them. Those people in developed countries who are excluded (or refuse to comply) and do not adopt the same consumption patterns are frowned upon. On the other hand, many of those who do adopt these patterns of conscious consumption are simply derided as hipsters, privileged or elitist urbanites. It looks like a post-modern version of the traditional class struggle.

The agendas of environmental groups today have also evolved quite considerable since their origins. Initially, they focused on issues such as water pollution, the use of pesticides, the protection of whales, the ban on atomic energy or the hole in the ozone layer. Today, the main goal for ecologists is to reduce CO_2 emissions caused by fossil fuels. This is a relatively recent demand, as is their intention to replace them with cleaner and renewable energies. We did not have the technology to do that in the past, but now it is possible to partially achieve it. As a consequence, our values about what is right and wrong have also changed. This is just another example of how the technology of any given society influences other practices, as well as its values and beliefs. We act and think the way we do partly because of the technologies that we have at that particular point in time.

For many of these environmental groups, the situation is so dire that they talk about a climate crisis or climate emergency. In their opinion, the consequences derived from global warming imply a climate change with disastrous repercussions such as extinction of species, desertification, destruction of crops, extreme changes in temperature, floods, plagues, etc. In order to avoid this apocalyptic scenario they demand a strong and immediate response from politicians at a global scale. Their presence on social media and in the press is seemingly permanent, with campaigns in support of the environmental cause. Public protests are also the norm and usually they are very well organised with actions that have international coverage and repercussions.

Most politicians know that this is not a spontaneous movement that will disappear in just a few months so they are conscious of the movement's power and influence. Public figures are forced to take action and show greater concern for the cause, sometimes out of conviction and sometimes out of obligation[14].

Nature was seen as indestructible during the days of the Soviet Union.

This is how we arrived at the climate summit in September 2019, an event organised by the UN in New York to discuss matters concerning the environment. In less time than the five minutes that her speech lasted, a very young Greta Thunberg simultaneously showed the sadness and the anger of a generation that has grown up under the anguish and anxiety of an apocalyptic future: *'How dare you! You have stolen my dreams and my childhood'*. The media made her a spokesperson for a generation that openly declared that the future of the planet is their greatest concern.

---

14. An obligation to be seen to be taking action.

Conflicting opinions

It is important to mention that not everyone shares this pessimistic view of the current situation. Those who criticise environmentalists argue that it is only natural if young people feel this anguish. They say that from schools and social media, they have constantly been indoctrinated in an ecological fundamentalism that is based on fear and catastrophism. There is not much difference between the messianic messages of environmentalist and the announcements of the end of the world by any religious cult. Nor does it seem that these young (and not so young) people really understand the social and economic implications that would come from eliminating fossil fuels entirely. If not managed in a phased and gradual manner, the geopolitical repercussions would be enormous. Most likely, they could lead to conflicts between countries that, in turn, would waste resources on weapons that could destroy societies and natural ecosystems at a much faster pace than global warming. Paradoxically, this is also a bleak reflection of the future, just like the one they criticise, but the events after the invasion of Ukraine by Russia seem to prove them right, at least partially.

Some critics see conformity in the attitude of the many youngsters who protest in the streets or go on strike in their universities and schools. They feel that many of young protesters today are not rebelling against anything; on the contrary, they are zealots of the mainstream ideas. They seem to be more conservative than the generations before them. Ultimately, it is said, it is only a pose because their claims are inconsistent with their lifestyle and consumption levels. Their mobile phones contradict their chants. Some, pressured by the dominant ideology of the moment, feel the need to repeat the slogans they have been taught. Everything is done in the name of a good cause that cannot be argued. To question, even partially, that ideological discourse is, in their opinion, to collaborate with the destruction of the planet.

Both positions are very conflicting in a debate that is one of the thorniest of today. So much so that most people prefer to avoid discussing the issue and ignore any type of argument against their position. Both sides claim to speak in the name of science and they are convinced of having data to prove their points. Obviously, in a climate of ideological warfare like this, it is very difficult to reach any consensus at all.

Some opinions are notoriously extreme. I have already mentioned some 'ecological fundamentalism' but at the polar opposite, among certain conservative Evangelist circles in the US, there is a theory that global warming is not so bad. In the words of John MacArthur (himself an evangelical pastor):

If you are going to vote for something, vote for warming. Less death due to cold, regions more habitable, larger crops, larger growing season. That's good. Warming helps the poor.

Fortunately for everyone, other positions are more moderate, but it is impossible to ignore the fact that there is an ideology at the base of them all. If we are going to have some degree of light on this debate it is necessary to clarify two things. The first one is whether nature is a strong or fragile system. The second is whether human beings are just another species or rather in a league of their own? Stated differently, before we enter in the debate we need to be aware of what our initial assumptions are, and to do that we need to answer these two questions:

1. What do we mean when we talk about *'nature'*?
2. What special position (if any) do human beings occupy in the world around us?

Nature as a strong system

The very idea of nature is extremely complex and confusing, but it can be viewed in two main ways in the context of this debate. The first one is a vision of nature as something inexhaustible. Nature, under this view, would be something that is practically indestructible. Thus, nature is capable of recovering from any aggression that human beings may exert.

This is the prevalent idea that communist countries inherited from their main ideologues (Karl Marx and Friedrich Engels). We can find plenty of evidence in the Soviet Union and satellite countries, as they saw nature as a resource to be exploited. This mentality led to numerous abuses and ecological disasters, such as the massive levels of air pollution, the shrinking of Aral Sea or the Chernobyl nuclear disaster. Paradoxically, the concern for the environment is generally associated with left-wing political movements (many of them of Marxist ideology), but in reality, this is a much more recent phenomenon. In its origins, there was no such concern about nature coming from the left nor right.

James Lovelock (1919-2022) was a British scientist and author who developed the interesting Gaia hypothesis. This theory is in tune with the vision of nature as a strong system. For Lovelock, planet Earth is a complex system where organisms, both living and inert, affect each other. We all evolve together to reach a state of equilibrium that helps perpetuate living conditions on the planet. Lovelock referred to planet

Earth as 'Gaia' in reference to the motherly Greek goddess. For Lovelock, it was clear that Gaia has an ultimate goal: to maintain ideal conditions for the development and conservation of life. This goal would affect everything: the atmosphere, ocean currents, seasonal cycles, living organisms, the number of individuals of each species, etc. According to this theory, if the human species were to become a danger to the balance of the system as a whole, the planet would get rid of us in the same way that a living organism gets rid of a virus. Gaia would devise a 'vaccine' to eliminate human beings, should they pose a real danger. Otherwise, it would continue to tolerate humans and even collaborate with them.

Gaia, the Greek goddess as 'Mother Nature'

In an interview with James Lovelock in his later years, he was asked what conditions would be like at the end of the 21st century. His answer was:

If we follow the 55 million years ago precedent, temperature rise will now be levelling off as the Earth's system -what I call Gaia- takes control. Just like when one of us gets a fever, our temperature doesn't go up until we become roast meat. It levels off at a higher level and after a while it sinks again.

This position does not deny the existence of climate change but rather tries to relativise the supposed climate emergency in which the planet finds itself. The problem is that of human beings, but Gaia will be fine, thank you! The Earth has already suffered numerous climatic changes much more extreme than the current one, and it clearly was not the end of the world.

Let's be clear on this: planet Earth has no problem, at least not a problem that we can solve. The problem is ours. What is in danger right now is the continuity of our society and lifestyle as we know it, not the planet's biodiversity in the medium or long term.

Controversially enough, Lovelock was also in favour of nuclear power as the only viable (and clean) alternative to using fossil fuels. According to Lovelock, the issue with nuclear power was its bad press. He looked at the areas where there have been nuclear disasters before and observes that in those places life continued as usual in a matter of only a few years. The risk of not using nuclear power is greater than the risk of using it. For him, it was a simple calculation of costs and benefits: the result is always favourable for using nuclear energy: it is the cheapest and most efficient of all forms of energy available to us.

Lovelock was not the only academic who felt this way about nuclear alternatives. Steven Pinker, for example, has a similar opinion about the benefits of nuclear energy. Given our current technology and safety measures, nuclear power can solve more problems than it creates.

Some criticise that children are used in protests.

If we continue exploring this idea of nature as an inexhaustible source, we can find an even tougher line. Some circles question that we can have clear evidence regarding global warming or climate change as a result of human action. Various groups (some scientist included) do not believe that there is definitive evidence that CO_2 is connected to extreme weather events and natural disasters because, in reality, climate change is a natural process in which humans do not intervene. Throughout many evolutionary cycles, Earth suffered climatic changes and phenomena that now we call natural disasters because they affect us: glaciations, global warming, droughts, rains, fires, etc. These phenomena also occurred in a time when there was no industrial activity and no human beings.

To consider this phenomenon as a disaster is not something that can be called scientific. It is simply and purely an egocentric view from a human perspective. We measure natural phenomena only as they affect us and do not consider the broader context of the planet. Even authors like Zygmunt Bauman[15] (1925-2017) refer to this in the following terms:

...the new concern for environmental issues owes its popularity to the widespread perception of the existence of a connection between the predatory misuse of the common resources of the planet and the threat that this could pose to the smooth development of the egocentric activities of our life.

However, it seems undeniable that some kind of global warming is taking place because the Keeling curve is there for everyone to see. What these critics are not prepared to accept is that all natural disasters are directly linked to the actions of human beings. To prove their point, they argue that some theories of the environmentalists are designed to always be right and hold humans responsible for any natural event that goes outside the norm. Environmentalists often see themselves as the crusaders fighting to protect us from destruction.

It is also very interesting to see how the most extreme views are also linked to political ideologies on many occasions. The general consensus is that conservative parties still advocate for the industrial and polluting *'old economy'*. However, liberal parties would prefer making the transition to *clean energy*, a sort of a new 'green capitalism'. They are best represented by technology companies, which are the main players of the *new economy*. These companies have seen an enormous opportunity to grow by taking advantage of this situation. The technology industry has generated an ideology based on its own

---

15. Zygmunt Bauman was a Polish sociologist and philosopher. He lived in England from 1971, where he studied at the London School of Economics and became Professor of Sociology at the University of Leeds, later Emeritus.

interests. This situation has created two camps: one formed by those who want to continue selling fossil fuels, and the other formed by those who want to sell electric cars, solar panels and wind turbines.

Nature as a fragile system

The opposite idea to nature as a strong system is that of nature as a fragile entity that needs constant care. During Romanticism in the nineteenth century, there was a vision of nature as something immense and sublime that dwarfs humans by comparison. In the paintings and literature of the moment, it was common to find images of big skies, storms on the high seas, inaccessible mountains, massive waves in the ocean etc. Mother Nature had become Step-Mother Nature. However, that idea has changed today. Human beings and nature are now considered to be on an equal footing. We could even say that we are in a position of advantage since we are more than seven billion human beings. Nature can annihilate us as individuals, but as a species, human beings can annihilate the whole planet.

This constant threat to the balance of life on the planet paints a bleak picture of the future. It marks the end of the utopia and optimism of modernity and rationalism. For centuries, the future was considered to be always better than the past; however, the post-modern mentality realises that the constant technological and scientific progress does not always lead us to a better world. Sometimes, unintended consequences may occur and it is Mother Nature who pays the piper.

This way of thinking, however, highlights the second question that we should address if we want to have a better idea of the positions that dominate the debate on climate change. The question is to determine what position human beings have in the world. Are we part of nature or are we something different? That is to say, isn't everything that is human also natural, including what humans produce, for example, factories, airplanes or farm fields?

The human being: West vs East

The question about humanity's place in the world does not have a single answer since it varies depending on the time and the type of society formed by these human beings.

However, at the risk of giving an overly simplistic image of a complex reality, we could schematically state that there are two main positions on this matter.

The first one refers to the idea of human beings as understood in Western societies (and by 'Western' I mean the classical Greek, Roman and Judeo-Christian tradition). In this tradition, the human being occupies a higher place in the cosmos. Although surrounded by nature, in reality, humans are something different from it. They are not an animal species like the others, but are the chosen ones, closer to the gods than to apes.

Since ancient times the classification of nature had been made into three kingdoms: the mineral, the vegetable and the animal. Subsequently, and as biological science advanced, new ones were added such as protista, fungi, bacteria, protozoa, chromista, etc.

Similarly, the realm of humans is also considered to be different from other species because only humans have a soul, or what we today call consciousness. According to this tradition, humans and nature are in constant conflict. Climate change is just another example of this difficult and dialectical relationship. Human beings, in their evolution, have moved away and protected themselves from the kingdom of nature, mainly by creating the 'kingdom of culture' and that includes things like houses, roads, science, trains, schools, central heating, Coca-Cola, etc. Consciously or not, this distinction between nature and culture is permanently present in the discussions about climate change. It is not the object of this book, but it would be very interesting to analyse the dualism of nature vs culture within this context.

On the opposite side of the spectrum, the Eastern tradition, prevails a different view of human beings and their position in the world. In many Eastern religions like Taoism, Buddhism or Hinduism, there is no clear distinction between man and nature. What really exists is a whole, a superior entity that surrounds them. Unlike in the West, there is no clear difference between human beings, plants or animals. They are all part of the same thing, an abstract entity that is greater than the sum of its parts.

This way of thinking about human beings goes hand in hand with an ethical position where the ultimate goal in life is to seek harmony between both ends (the human and the nature). It is also quite easy to find modulations of this thinking in many environmental groups of western societies. As we saw before, they are directly or indirectly influenced by 'orientalism'. Quite often, these ideas about nature and human beings are also linked to practices such as vegetarianism, yoga, veganism, transcendental meditation or spiritualism. All of them are more implanted in the East but are increasingly present in other countries as an alternative to Western practices.

Conclusion

As can be deduced from all the above, the idea of nature is a rather metaphysical one. What is more, from an ontological point of view, there is no such thing as 'Earth climate' taken as a whole. There is not "a climate", what exists are different climates spread over different regions of the planet. Generalisations cannot be easily made about climate because it is a non-operative idea; climate cannot be studied as a metaphysical entity. Climate change is a murky idea but one that is so present in our daily life that it is impossible to ignore. However nebulous this idea is, it is indisputable that it has a real influence on the way we think and act. In the name of climate change budgets can be altered, taxes increased, movements restricted, crops limited, diets altered, etc.

Ideology is important when interpreting any phenomena, as it is clearly the case when debating about climate change. We cannot separate our theoretical assumptions from our political or social positions since all are closely linked. However, regardless of the ideology of each group or individual, if we want the strategies to tackle climate change to be effective and significantly reduce the levels of CO_2 in the atmosphere, decisions have to be made on a larger scale. It is useless if, for example, Germany passes 'green legislation' whilst other countries continue to increase their emissions.

On a different note, the appropriateness of using children in protests, demonstrations and strikes under the guise of 'saving the planet' is to be questioned. It is not the planet that is in danger but our way of life, the world as we know it, but not the world in itself. Even if the average temperature increases by 10 degrees Celsius in the future, the planet will continue to move around the sun with an enormous variability of species.

Obviously, no one wants this to happen, but we should at least be more rigorous about the messages that we make public.

The task of Philosophy is very uncomfortable as it has to "patrol" the intellectual consistency of any debate, let alone one as passionate as climate change. Little wonder that for this very reason many people do not like it.

CHAPTER 8

SEX, GENDER & DESIRE

'One is not born,
but rather becomes a woman.'

(Simone de Beauvoir)

Discussion

It has become clear for quite a while that biological sex and gender are two different things, but are they the only alternatives that define the sexual identity of an individual? What does it mean that gender is fluid and how does it affect us? How has post-modern philosophy deconstructed the binary positions 'male/female' and 'masculine/feminine'? Do feminists and transexuals have a common agenda or are there irreversible conflicts between them?

Introduction

There are very few sportspeople who have been more successful than the British boxer Lennox Lewis (1965). Gold medalist at the Seoul 88 Olympic Games and several times heavyweight champion of the world, some experts consider him the best boxer in his category. At 1.96 metres tall and weighing 111 kg with an impressive range of movements, the truth is that there are many reasons to believe that.

In order to have a great career and succeed in the boxing world, both the physical condition and the talent of the boxer are essential. However, to be internationally recognised as the best, Lennox also needed a top-notch agent and an excellent promoter. Frank Maloney (b.1953) was the right person for the job, and he took the British boxer's career to the top.

In his youth, Frank Maloney toyed with the idea of being a boxer himself, but it was hard to earn a living as a professional pugilist. Soon, he realised that he needed a plan B and started training other boxers. Then, almost naturally, he began promoting fights until he became Lennox Lewis's agent in 1989. Together, they had a long and successful career. Certainly, those were very good years, financially and professionally speaking. Yet, deep down inside his mind, Frank Maloney knew something was very wrong.

After Lennox Lewis retired, Frank tried his hand at politics. He ran for mayor of London in the 2004 local election. He was a member of the right-wing and nationalist party, UKIP, best known for its anti-European hardline and for being staunch advocates of Brexit, among many other controversial things.

During his political campaign, Frank Maloney appeared several times in the media making very negative comments about homosexuals. Among other things, he made statements such as:

I don't want to campaign around gays...I don't think they do a lot for society.

I'm not homophobic, but in public let's live a proper moral life – I think that's important.

I'm more for traditional family values and family life. I'm anti-same-sex marriages, and I'm anti-same-sex families'.

If you are homosexual, you are homosexual – just get on with your life and stop bitching about things.

His opinions, expressed in 2004 were not unusual within a large sector of society. Simply put, Frank Maloney was voicing a judgement that many citizens, even in the most liberal countries, kept private.

Frank's remarks on this matter would have no relevance whatsoever if it weren't for what happened next. After finishing fourth in the elections with 6.2% of the votes, his life took a spectacular turn. Gone were two marriages and three children. The time had come to be honest and accept something that, for him, was a source of internal conflict. Frank Maloney actually felt like a woman trapped in a man's body. However, he lived in a very masculine environment and had to repress himself. Some years later, in 2014, Frank publicly announced that he suffered from gender dysphoria and was changing genders. Her name from that moment on would be Kellie Maloney. A year later, she successfully completed the sex change operations that culminated in a long and tortuous journey.

At this point, it is understandable to ask: how this was even possible? What happened to cause such a radical change in this person's life?

The change of post-modernity

To understand what happened, it is not enough to give a psychological answer, nor just attribute everything to the personal circumstances of Kellie Maloney. In the first place, it should be pointed out that what we have experienced is a gradual change in society's attitude as a whole, or at least in the society in which Kellie Maloney lives. In recent years there has been a greater acceptance and permissiveness so Kellie Maloney can walk through the streets without the fear of being harassed by the authorities and her fellow citizens (something that would have happened only a few decades ago). Today, not only she is relatively safe, she is also very popular participating in very popular television contests.

However, if we really want to understand how this change(s) in values has occurred and how we accept something that would be impossible a few years ago, we have to refer to the role of post-modern philosophy. In particular, we must mention the consequences derived from the theory of deconstruction, as elaborated by Jacques Derrida (1930–2004).

The concept of deconstruction is inspired by the project of another twentieth century philosopher, Martin Heidegger (1889-1976). His goal, as he announced in his 1924 work *Being and Time*, was the destruction of all metaphysics. He intended to eliminate the traditional way of thinking in philosophy since classical Greece. Derrida avoided using the term 'destruction' because it sounded too strong. It was not about destroying but about overcoming an artificial opposition, and that is why he coined the term *'deconstruction'*.

The difference could be seen in the use of Lego. One can build a house with the different pieces and think that it is a "natural" or "logical" construction. Derrida preferred to disas-

semble the pieces that made up the house because taken sep-
arately, there was nothing in nature that makes them a house.
Those same pieces could form a car or a bus. Actually, the
strong thesis of post-modernity is that there is no nature of
things; everything could be otherwise.

Young Sicilian man dressed as a Spanish woman in the late 19th century.

'Deconstruction' is a philosophical theory that focuses on
the analysis of traditional binary oppositions: the masculine
and the feminine, the good and the bad, the body and the
soul, the left and the right, life and death, etc. For Derrida,
these are metaphysical oppositions; that is, they seek to re-

duce the enormous complexity of the world into two pairs of opposites. Those are only artificial and very limiting divisions that lack a foundation and therefore are susceptible to being deconstructed.

Generally speaking, in these binary oppositions, there is a dominant element (for example, the masculine) and another element that is dominated (the feminine). This division establishes a violent hierarchy between the two terms in opposition. The aim of post-modern philosophy is to overcome this situation. However, Derrida did not want to reverse that hierarchy and put the previously dominated element as the dominator because we would fall into the same violent hierarchy that we were trying to avoid. What deconstruction aims to do is weaken the strength of the opposition, destabilise the belief in that hierarchy, prove it unjustified and over simplistic. There is no masculine and feminine as such, but one could speak of a 'fluidity' or even an 'instability'.

This theory of deconstruction has had enormous success. First, it was gaining followers in academic fields, and later its implications became evident in many areas of society. Proof of its popularity is the fact that the term 'deconstruction' began to be applied in fields as different as literature, politics and gastronomy.

Sex and gender: fluidity

Until very recently, almost no one questioned the idea that there are only two biological sexes (male and female). Associated with each one of them are two genders (masculine and feminine). Males display a behaviour that is considered masculine, and females exhibit a behaviour that is called feminine.

When this is not the case, and a male adopts the role of the female (or vice versa), they are considered deviant individuals. It is also true that these deviations from the norm are relatively frequent in history, and in the best of cases, they have been tolerated. In most cases, however, they have been repressed and punished.

The idea that there are more than two sexes and only two genders is something much more recent. It is also a very far-reaching matter with implications in many aspects of our society. To accept that there are actually more than two sexes means blowing up the traditional binary opposition between male and female. This is the reason why in recent times we have started talking of 'fluidity'.

Today it is no longer necessary for a person to identify as 'male or female'. In fact, they can be both to different degrees. The identity of an individual depends on factors such as biology, age, social context, the circle of friends, education, religion or even when a person can decide on a whim, Moreover, it would not make any sense to consider that there is a 'natural' masculine or feminine way of dressing, acting, speaking, gesturing or thinking. Simone de Beauvoir (1908–1986) summed it up by saying that a woman is not born but is made. Being a woman or a man is no longer associated with gender. Gender is a cultural construction, not a natural one (although the distinction between 'nature' and 'culture' is quite confusing too).

The philosopher Judith Butler (1956) started from the same idea as Simone de Beauvoir; however, she extended it to any gender role. According to Butler, gender identity is constructed through some type of statements called *performative* Performative statements are those that, when they are said, transform the reality they mention. It's like doing things with words. For example, when a jury says, '*You are guilty*', there is a transformation in the 'real' world; these are words that have consequences. It is something more than merely saying or describing; it is changing reality using words. Other examples of performative acts would be *'I declare you husband and wife'* or *'You are fired'*.

For Butler, even before a baby is born, there is an authorised person, usually a doctor who 'performatively' assigns the baby one of the two sexes. Consequently, doctors assign performatively a gender to the foetus when they announce they are to be parents: *'It is a girl.'* From that moment, and before being born, the future baby has already been assigned a specific sex and a role. Subsequently, parents, family, school and society, continue with this process of 'formation' in womanhood through statements such as *'Boys use this toilet and girls use the other'*, *'Blue is for boys and pink is for girls'* and so many other examples. In her essay *Performative Acts and Gender Constitution* Judith Butler states that:

> ...*gender is in no way a stable identity or locus of agency from which various acts proceed; rather, it is an identity tenuously constituted in time -an identity instituted through a stylized repetition of acts. Further, gender is instituted through the stylization of the body and, hence, must be understood as the mundane way in which bodily gestures, movements, and enactments of various kinds constitute the illusion of an abiding gendered self. This formulation moves the conception of gender off the ground of a substantial model of identity to one that requires a conception of a constituted social temporality. (…) a constructed identity, a performative accomplishment which the mundane social audience, including the actors themselves, come to believe and to perform in the mode of belief. If the ground of gender identity is the stylized repetition of acts through time, and not a seemingly seamless iden-*

tity, then the possibilities of gender transformation are to be found in the arbitrary relation between such acts, in the possibility of a different sort of repeating, in the breaking or subversive repetition of that style.

Currently, biological science and medicine have opened the door to a greater variability in the sex of any given individual. To the traditional 'male' or 'female' is added the 'intersex gender' (sometimes called 'hermaphrodite'). There is also variability in this third gender and we can have an intersex gender with female characteristics and an intersex gender with masculine characteristics. This division can give a better account of a reality that was previously too narrow. The previous dualism was considered restrictive because it left out a significant number of individuals who did not identify themselves as male or female.

Masculine	Non-binary	Feminine
Male	Intersex	Female
	Intersex with masculine characteristics	
	Intersex with feminine characteristics	

A more inclusive identification with a sex.

Desire

Following in the wake of post-modern philosophy (especially that of Derrida and Foucault), other authors such as Paul B. Preciado (1970) introduced a third element in the matrix: 'desire'. The sexual identity of an individual is formed not only by their gender and biological sex, but also by their desire. Sexual desire can go in any direction. The number of possibilities is enormous and not necessarily permanent (it can change through life). For instance, someone like Kellie Maloney may have been born biologically as a male and be attracted to women. Later in life this person identifies as female, exhibit feminine behaviours and desire men. However, in the future she could also desire women again, intersex individuals or exclusively other transgender people in her situation. The diversity of choice is wider now and not necessarily binding, it can evolve over time.

Drag Ball in a club in New York. The shows in which men dressing up as women were a hit in the 1920s.

Accordingly, since there are no binary restrictions, we must accept that there is fluidity also in our desire. The resulting variability is enormous and not reducible to simple dualisms. The previous paradigm is now considered to be binary, violent in its authoritarian, limiting, artificial and repressive. In this sense, we can say that the opposition 'masculine/feminine' has been deconstructed because it has been overcome. Biological sex, gender and desire are left open to variability. They are not closed categories because, throughout our biography, we can fluctuate from one side of the spectrum to the other, and hence the use of the adjective 'fluid'.

Historically, sexual desire has been considered a more personal and subjective question, For example, among the ancient Greeks, it was well regarded for an older man to have sex with young males. And in the prisons of the United States, consensual sex between prisoners of the same sex is common currency, although very few inmates would consider themselves homosexual or bisexual.

Authors like Paul B. Preciado (*née* Beatriz Preciado) are trying to make sexual desire independent of the 'dictatorship of the binary'. Desire should not be limited to a specific biological sex or gender, either. Anyone with certain characteristics, regardless of sex or gender, could be desired. The bottom line here is that one desires a person with certain traits regardless of their sex or gender. Biology does not necessarily condition our desires.

Different types of societies

Traditionally, biological sex and gender roles have been considered something objective, that is, something 'natural'. The big shift we have experienced in recent years is that now they are viewed as purely subjective. This subjectivity fits perfectly in our liberal-capitalist societies, where individual freedom and subjectivity are not only tolerated but in fact celebrated. The categories of sex, gender and desire acquire the status of commodities in a capitalist market. If we can freely choose between various types of cereals, something similar happens with the categories we have been considering here. Identity, in a free-market capitalist society, is largely established by consumption. An individual distinguishes from (or identifies with) other individuals through the products and services that they consume. This is the reason why consuming is so important for teenagers who are forming their personalities and creating 'an identity'.

It happens, however, that in more homogeneous or egalitarian societies, *deviations* from the norm cannot be easily tolerated. In countries like China and in most ex-communist countries, sex and gender are also public issues. Sexual practices and preferences are therefore a political matter not merely a private issue. It would be inconceivable that an individual could alter their sex or their gender roles without disrupting society as a whole. In fact, that is precisely what authorities are trying to avoid. In the case of China, for instance, the changes have to be controlled by the Chinese Communist Party, not by the individual decisions of the citizens. This does not mean that sexual relations between people of the same sex do not exist in China (they obviously do), but they are generally clandestine, and each individual usually plays the role assigned to their gender: father, mother, housewife, grandparent, etc.

In other countries, like Thailand, it is accepted that there is a third gender. It is not masculine or feminine, it is called *kathoeys* and derogatorily known in English as *ladyboys*. They are transexual males who take the role that Thai society typically assign to women. They are an essential part of the society and are accepted even by Buddhist monks.

In some Native American societies there is also the acceptance of a third gender: *berdaches*. They are men dressed in female clothes offering sexual gratification to male warriors.

However, they are not excluded from their society; on the contrary, they are regular members who fulfil a role as important as any other.

All these examples are only evidence of the huge variability already existing in the world. They are also helpful to put in perspective the presumed originality of some modern claims regarding sex, gender, desire and identity.

Queer Theory

In some western countries, the academic discipline that deals with the study of gender and 'non-normative' sexual practices (that is, those that are not heterosexual) is known as 'Queer Theory'. The term 'queer' can be understood in this context as 'deviant', and it is opposed to "straight". Therefore, the focus is on the study of the practices that go outside the imposed norm.

These academic studies are based on the idea, developed by Michel Foucault (1926–1984), that not only is gender a social construction, but sexual desire and sexual practices also are. We behave the way we have been taught to behave, and that depends on the sex we are assigned at birth. In the same way, we desire those people who we have been taught to desire, and this is also conditioned by factors such as race, education, social class, etc. Any type of deviation from the established norm must be 'corrected'. The institutions that can 'correct' x this deviation are schools, hospitals, churches, science, or prisons. They all are part of a larger system of power that seeks to impose a certain morality always in line with the preservation of that power. In many countries it is taught in school that homosexuality is bad. Many churches preach that only men and women can form a family. Prisons in many islamic countries are full of "sexual deviants" who put in risk the good order of society.

In our post-modern society though, many of these institutions of power have accepted, and assimilated, as 'normal' something that previously was considered a 'deviation'. In a twisted way, we could say that deviations have become 'the new normal'. In many schools they teach students the importance of accepting the sexual orientations of their peers. Many churches are beginning to publicly accept homosexuals among their members, and hospitals have sex clinics where groups of individuals considered to be at risk (sexual workers, for instance) are informed and advised on sexual diseases regardless of their orientation or practices.

In relatively recent times (but especially since the 1990s), social movements such as LGTBQI+ have grown considerably. Together with some other 'traditional' social rights movements such as feminism, they began to exert an influence that many people today see with concern. Following Foucault's maxim *where there is power, there is resistance*, these movements originally arose as opposition to a certain type of stablished power. Once they have been assimilated and accepted, they become a new power and, consequently, they generate resistance against them. In many countries, groups that fight for the rights of gays or transsexuals are received with hostility, not because of the sexual practices they observe but because of the power they can wield in changing many aspects of society (such as family values, fairness in competitive sports, new marriage laws, the use of inclusive language, new labour laws, etc.). After seeing the power they have accumulated, opposition groups have decided to wage a cultural but also political battle to balance their power.

Conflict of interests

It is also necessary to consider these LGTBQI+ collectives in a broader context. They are often included in a more general movement where the main goal is the defence of marginalised and oppressed members of society. These less fortunate groups would include ethnic or religious minorities, homosexuals, transexuals, women, political dissidents, sex workers, undocumented immigrants, etc.

However, and contrary to what many might think of the situation, it cannot be said that these groups have a common agenda. Their interests and beliefs are constantly in a state of conflict. For instance, some minorities are oppressed because of their religion, but that same religion does not tolerate homosexuality or puts women in a position that is far from acceptable for any type of feminist movement.

Even within feminism, there are two opposing views: one is known as 'feminism of equality', and the other as 'feminism of difference' (also called 'essentialist'). Schematically, it could be said that the first type fights to achieve equal rights and opportunities in all areas of society. The second type of feminism is an in-depth critique of all the knowledge produced by society at large: science, literature, medicine, philosophy, psychology, etc. This particular line of thought believes that knowledge is dominated by what they consider to be a 'hetero-patriarchy'. This means that all sexual practices, moral values, scientific studies, academic research and generally every relationship between people are dictated by heterosexual men who have not taken into account the view of women (much less homosexual women).

This 'feminism of difference' is also called 'essentialist' because they claim that there is an essence of being a woman and an essence of being a man. Quite obviously, this thinking goes against the 'feminism of equality' since the equality that they defend implies the refusal to admit that a woman is an essence. Let's remember Simone de Beauvoir's idea that women are not born but made through education and society.

The more radical 'feminism of difference' is also in full conflict with the transsexual community among many others. By emphasising the difference between men and women, it cannot be admitted that men like Frank Maloney can change their gender at will. Otherwise, the specificity of women would be eliminated if we allow men to change their gender, and that is precisely what they are fighting against.

Today, the idea that desire, sex and gender are fluid is widespread. This new tolerant attitude is increasingly accepted in schools and other institutions of power. However, we cannot ignore the fact that this idea is also challenged and criticised by other groups in our society. The biggest opposition usually comes from organised religions. They argue that if the world (including all animals and human beings) has been created by God, reversing that natural order is going against a divine law. It would be arrogant and far away from religious morality to alter the traditional role of men and women in matters of sex, gender or desire.

We should not overlook the fact that even in more tolerant western societies there is still great reluctance in many places to grant full rights to homosexuals and transexuals. For instance, the issue of adoption is still quite controversial, and in many countries, if not all, homosexual and bisexual individuals cannot donate blood, or at least they have to wait between three months to one year depending on the country.

Conclusion

The current debate on the fluidity of the sexes and genders has exploded some conceptions associated with gender roles and sexual desire.

It has also allowed many people who did not identify themselves with any of the previous categories to feel more comfortable and integrated. Furthermore, it has opened the possibility to other forms of identification that go beyond sexual preferences or gender roles.

However, if we accept that biological sex does not determine the identity of the person, then, someone who was born with the biological traits of a male can identify as a female. This is relatively normal in today's society, but why should we stop here and not go even further? If biology does not determine identity, can someone whose parents are from different races identify as black or white person? Is the concept of race also somewhat fluid? And what about the concept of being human? Is it also something fluid? Can someone be more or less human? In fact, there are many people who believe they are trapped in a human body but they actually feel like they are dogs or cats or mermaids.

These kinds of questions might sound ridiculous to many, but they are relevant not only today, they will be even more pertinent in years to come as technology evolves. Let's not forget that most of our ideas and beliefs are full of contradictions or they simply are not as rooted as we might think. However, that does mean that our beliefs have to be ignored.

Undoubtedly, the recognition of the legal rights of the LGTBQI+ community is a necessary advance, but we must not ignore that it opens the possibility to other questions of identity that, taken to extremes, could lead to unacceptable contradictions (at least from the conception of the world that we have in the present).

There are many other factors that influence our attitude regarding issues such as homosexuality or feminism. In particular, the material conditions of existence of any given society, such as birth and death rates, diseases, the amount of resource available, the total number of the population, wars, etc.

These are all important factors when it comes to showing more or less permissiveness with issues such as sexual morality and tolerance towards gender fluidity.

CHAPTER 9

IDENTITY AND FRAGMENTATION

'The medium is the message.'
(Marshall McLuhan)

Discussion

Modern societies have always been formed by heterogenous groups but, it seems as if in recent years we have been fragmented more than ever before into identity groups that use gender, race, sexual orientation, etc. as the defining factor. Is this really as liberating as it looks or does it limit us even more? Are all these identity groups as clear and rational as they claim to be or are they based more on feelings and subjectivity? Also, if we had to assess our society today, are we in a better position than before? Can we say that we live in a better world, or on the contrary we have degenerated as a society and as a species?

Introduction

Dijon, France, 1750. The Academy of Arts and Sciences organises a competition open to everyone able to submit a serious academic essay about the proposed topic: 'If the establishment of the arts and sciences has contributed to improving customs.' Or translated into common parlance: 'Have science and art really made us better individuals? And have they produced a fairer society?'

Almost all the participants that took part in this prestigious competition answered in the affirmative. After all, was there any doubt that science had improved the quality of life? And who could deny that the arts allowed us to communicate and express ourselves on a deeper symbolic level?

This view also considers that it is thanks to science and art that we live a better life. They have made us morally better than before when we lived in a primitive stage of our evolution as human beings. Luckily, society today is no longer about the 'law of the jungle'. We have overcome that moment and now we live in a more elevated stage that is considerably better in many different ways.

The common assumption at the time was that we evolved historically and progressed toward an improved version of society as a whole. Besides, at the individual level, we have also improved as moral subjects. Put the other way around: the further we go back in time, the worse the material conditions and the more unfair and violent society was.

This type of mentality presupposes an idea of the human being in constant progress. As if we were climbing a ladder in which each rung is better than the previous one. The only thing debatable in 18th century was whether that ladder has infinite steps or whether there is a moment when the peak of historical evolution is reached. Is there a limit to the progress of humanity? Can we constantly improve as a species until we reach a point where we are no longer humans but a superior kind of entity?

Portrait of Rousseau (unknown author).

Despite the optimistic atmosphere, the winner of the contest, however, was an odd and cranky character who was opposed to the common view of his contemporaries. Shockingly, he thought that the arts and sciences had brought nothing but misery to our lives.

The author's name was Jean-Jacques Rousseau (1712–1778), and he believed that it would have been preferable if science and art had not advanced at all. He asserted that humanity would be better off had it remained in any previous phase of human evolution. In his opinion, the sciences and the arts were responsible for all evil, in particular they accounted for creating luxury and therefore, they were guilty of introducing inequality in society. Inequality was our biggest enemy and when this inequality was taken to the extreme it produced slavery. All these unwanted effects were the fault of the continuous development of the sciences and the arts. Whatever improvements they might have introduced in our lives, they would never make up for all the ills they produced.

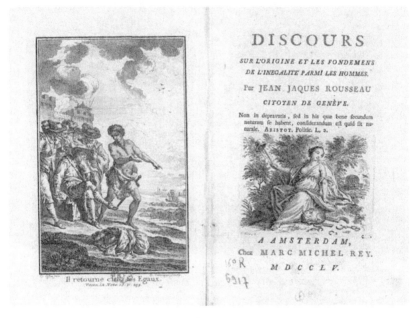

Speech on equality (Rousseau 1755).

Rousseau was convinced, on the other hand, that human beings in their primitive state were good and fair. Society, corrupted by the arts and sciences ended up destroying everything good and natural that existed in this primitive man.

Rousseau believed that the sciences, far from being academic disciplines with a noble origin as many regarded them, had an ostensibly vulgar and evil origin. Astronomy, for instance, was born from the superstition, deception and falsehood of astrology. Geometry was born from the greed of farmers in measuring and limiting their lands so as not to share them with anyone else. Physics, on the other hand, appeared simply because of the idleness, indolence and prying of some individuals with nothing better to do.

These ideas may seem naive to us from a distance and in fact they show a notable contradiction since on the one hand Rousseau believed that men were good by nature, but at the same time created and invented horrific things.

However, it should not be forgotten that Rousseau's ideas have exerted an enormous influence on later authors. For instance, it is easy to see the roots of Rousseau's thinking in many left-wing and also religious movements. Rousseau has been particularly influential in the field of pedagogy and in much of the curriculum renewal movement. He believed that schools should be teaching the students according to their own interests and not for mere academic rigour or discipline. Throughout history there have been many attempts to educate children using these ideas, although not always successfully.

It is also quite paradoxical that Rousseau, despite these liberal ideas, abandoned his five children in different orphanages and never took care of their education. Rousseau was undoubtedly a contradictory and difficult man. His biography is very unusual and worthy of a novel. It is full of false conversions, betrayals, lovers, abandonments, paranoia, poverty, fame…

Perhaps, as a result of all this, Rousseau was not exactly an optimist. He did not have a good opinion of the world around him nor did he have the impression that the future was necessarily going to be much better. In fact, Rousseau was advocating for a return to a state of nature that had been lost because of the evil influence of arts and sciences. After the publication of one of his books, the French philosopher Voltaire, who was also his intellectual rival, wrote him the following ironic letter:

I have received your new book against human race, and thank you for it. Never was such a cleverness used in the design of making us all stupid. One longs, in reading your book, to walk on all fours. But as I lost that habit for more than sixty years, I feel unhappily the impossibility of resuming it. Nor can I embark in search of the savages of Canada, because the maladies to which I am condemned render a European surgeon necessary to me; because war is going on in those regions; and because the example of our actions has made the savages nearly as bad as ourselves.

Reason, feelings and an earthquake in Lisbon

Rousseau lived during the Enlightenment, a historical period marked by confidence in reason and optimism for a better future. All this was happening thanks to scientific and technical progress. It was during this period that the sciences advanced enormously, for instance in the fields of economics, sociology, demography, geography and of course physics.

The general idea was that through scientific rationality, all the phenomena of the universe would be explained and, at the same time, humanity would become morally better. Reason, together with observation and experimentation, put human beings in control of physical phenomena for the first time in history. This empowerment over nature gave enormous optimism for the future.

There was one event in particular, however, that led to a profound change in mentality with regards to natural phenomena. It happened in Lisbon on the morning of November 1st, 1755. It had disastrous consequences in other places like Morocco or the south-eastern coast of Spain, but it was especially tragic in the Portuguese capital. A scale 9 earthquake with an epicentre in the Atlantic Ocean caused devastating damage to the city. It was not the first time that Lisbon was shaken by a major earthquake; in 1531 a scale 8 earthquake hit the capital. Both were disastrous, but the one in 1755 was especially so since forty minutes later a 3-wave tsunami arrived on the shores, devastating the port and the centre of the city where a large part of the population had sought refuge. To further complicate matters, Lisbon was full of candles lit in honour of the deceased: November 1st was All Saint's Day. For five days the buildings of the city burned until most of them were reduced to ashes.

The dramatic intensity of images increases with the rise of Romanticism.
'The Nightmare' (Henry Fuseli, 1781).

This major disaster had a huge effect on the European intelligentsia. It made some of their members wonder why God would punish innocent people and let churches built in His honour burn in a devout Christian country? Were we defenceless against natural phenomena like this? Was it possible to do something to protect ourselves in the future if something similar were to happen?

Enlightened thinkers believed that by scientific and rational means they could predict and cushion the effects of these types of phenomena. The Lisbon earthquake laid the foundation for the birth of modern seismology and the construction of earthquake resistant buildings. All these projects were under the direction of the enlightened Portuguese Sebastiao Melo[16] (1699-1782) who managed to clean the city of debris in just one year. His determination was summed up in his famous phrase: *'Now what? We bury the dead and feed the living.'* With this spirit, the new buildings were tested before the tremors with large groups of trotting soldiers to observe the effect they produced on the constructions.

This was the typical rational Enlightenment mindset. It relied on science and arts as protection against the elements, but Rousseau would have none of that. With him, the previous optimism ended, and a new historical period known as 'Romanticism' began. Authors started to question whether reason was the dominant element in life. Unlike the Enlightenment, Romanticism was extremely popular and spread like wildfire across Europe, being especially influential among the young.

According to romantic ideas, the deciding factor in both private and public (political) life should be the way we feel about things, not reason itself. It was not by chance that at this time nationalism started to spread, always based on sen-

---

16. known as the Marquis of Pombal , he was a Portuguese statesman and diplomat who effectively ruled the Portuguese Empire from 1750 to 1777 as chief minister to King Joseph I. He modernized the kingdom's administrative, economic, and ecclesiastical institutions. During his lengthy ministerial career, Pombal accumulated and exercised autocratic power.

timental concepts such as racial purity, soul, folklore, culture, tradition and identity.

It was also during this period that we can perceive a huge change in ethics. The things that were considered good or fair during Romanticism were no longer the same things as before. The aesthetics shifted a great deal too and now artists had different ideals and principles, such as romantic beauty, love, race, nature or a deep feeling of communion with something divine that was in the innermost part of everyone. These were all very intangible and subjective ideas. Also, with Romanticism, it became acceptable to appeal to a feeling inside our hearts to justify almost any cause instead of using rational arguments. Today, we are experiencing something similar in Western societies, as we will see.

During the previous period - the rationalism of the Enlightenment - the deciding factor was a logical or mathematical deduction. Not anymore. Romanticism appealed to feelings of the heart. It is actually hard to understand what that means because Romanticism deals with feelings, not with meanings. It was not about understanding the world around us, instead it was about feeling the world inside of us. The philosophy of Immanuel Kant (1724–1804) is a good example of this transition between Enlightenment and Romanticism. He tried to account for these two elements (rationality and sentiment) in a very systematic and academic way. On one hand he put clear boundaries to knowledge in his Critique of the Pure Reason (1781)[17]. On the other, he had to introduce some element of 'emotion' in his Critique of the Practical Reason (1788).

---

17. At the foundation of Kant's system is the doctrine of 'transcendental idealism,' which emphasizes a distinction between what we can experience (the natural, observable world) and what we cannot ('supersensible' objects such as God and the soul). Kant argued that we can only have knowledge of things we can experience.

The present time

As we have seen, the transition from the Enlightenment to Romanticism brought enormous changes. It represented a shift in values, ideals, goals, attitudes, etc. In short, it brought a new way of seeing the world and changed our relationship with it.

We could also draw a parallel between that shift and the present time. The social changes of the last decades can be seen as a second transition from the Enlightenment to Romanticism. We have shifted from a time of trust and optimism in scientific and technological progress to a new time dominated by disenchantment and mistrust.

After the fall of the Soviet Union in the late 1980s and early 1990s, there was a transition (at times more intended than real) towards Western-style liberal capitalist democracies. This period coincides with a spectacular development in computer science. Many households were able to afford a personal computer. At the same time, mobile phones became ubiquitous. Genetic science began to show spectacular results with the Human Genome Project and medical scientists were optimistic about cures for many diseases.

It was also at that same time that international flights became fabulously cheap. Many were able to afford two holidays a year in destinations that until recently would have been considered exclusive for the upper classes.

The rise of the internet made information available anywhere in the world in real time. We gained access to all public libraries, along with the possibility of contacting people from other continents in a matter of seconds (and almost always free of charge) all thanks to email.

These circumstances encouraged optimism as they made our future a utopian place. Everything new was considered not only good but also beautiful. We only need to watch at any Apple presentation of that time to see how their products became the standard in quality and aesthetics. Technology was not only useful, it was beautiful and also good. All inequalities would soon disappear as more technological devices and applications developed. The day would come when we would hardly have to work because robots would do it for us. Wars and conflicts would be reduced to a minimum as we would all be united in what was called the "global village", fuelled by free markets in increasing freer societies.

The population would have access to information that was previously inaccessible and, consequently, we could make better political decisions. Doubtless, the behaviour of citizens would improve and crime rates would be minimised. Thanks to chat rooms and social media, people would not feel lonely anymore. Meeting our soul mates would be somewhat easier since the number of potential suitors increased exponentially; if it was something scientific, there was an algorithm to prove it.

During those decades, we were optimistic about the future, even if we did not know it at the time. There were, of course, critics of this optimism but the dominant mindset was generally positive. The year 2000 (after the initial fear of the so called 'Millennium bug') was greeted with a mixture of expectation and optimism for whatever technical advances it could bring. Computers, telephones, software, etc., were becoming better every year. By 2004 there was talk everywhere about Web 2.0, websites that emphasised user generated content. Everything now was more interactive and the lines between users, consumers, creators, sellers, companies, individuals, etc. completely blurred. It was the result of a major technological evolution, always towards something better despite the fact that the mood was already darkening after the 2001 terrorist attacks and the stock market crash of the technology companies known as the 'dot-com bubble'.

Internet users could interact and collaborate freely with each other as content creators: blogs, wikis, profiles, videos, audio, etc. The social media of the time, such as MySpace or Facebook, were seen as something new and positive. Thanks to them, we could be in contact with friends, relatives and people who lived far away. We could even meet someone new with similar interests and everything in the safety of our homes. Unlike today, almost no one questioned the benefits of these services. The social media companies of the time were platforms created to show our individuality to the rest of world – surely one of the greatest prizes of any liberal consumer society. Negative comments or extreme political arguments were not yet the norm.

However, as the new millennium advanced, it was clear that many expectations would never be met. In many cases, technological evolution brought with it a series of unwanted effects that questioned the initial optimism.

Many countries that transitioned from the Soviet bloc to capitalism managed to improve and stabilise their economic situation to some degree. However, new problems were generated, such as unemployment, political corruption (although this was hardly new), insecurity, cyber-crime or wars of independence like those of the Balkans and Chechnya.

In developed countries, the technology that was supposed to free us from the heaviest burdens ended up creating equally tedious tasks. E-mails eliminated the need to write elaborate letters; however, we began to spend much more time writing and reading irrelevant e-mails than we did before, not to mention the proliferation of scams that used e-mails as bait.

Liquid society

With the consolidation of social media and online newspapers we have experienced a gradual transition from platforms of information and entertainment to platforms of controversy. In many cases the hate was aimed at individuals or groups of a certain political ideology. This is especially obvious today in the section designated for comments where the anonymity of users means that the basic rules of communication are broken. Likewise, dating apps (although still popular), are now viewed with a certain distrust, and the sincerity of the profiles or the veracity of images is open to question. In hindsight, our initial positive attitude towards the future looks rather naive. We have been blinded by new technologies and the changes they promised to bring about to our societies. It seems clear now that the expectations were too high. Technology would not fix all our problems, in fact it can create its own.

Today, the younger generations claim to have the highest levels of stress, worried as they are about their negative perception of the future. The university of Bath, in collaboration with other universities, elaborated a survey among young people in UK, Finland, France, the US, Australia, Portugal, Brazil, India, the Philippines and Nigeria. The results were:

- 83% feel that we have failed to care for the planet.
- 75% thinks that the future is frightening.
- 65% believe that governments are failing young people.
- Only 31% think that governments can be trusted.

The so called "eco-anxiety" is the result of a bleak vision of the present and the future. They perceive that the environment deteriorates, natural disasters multiply, politics are destabilised, their prospects of getting a job that allows them to live like their parents diminish, the possibility of finding a stable and lasting partner is reduced by the abundance of choice and divorce rates, the fear of being 'cancelled' for saying something offensive or incorrect increases. The impartiality of justice is questioned. There is suspicion of police action and, generally speaking, there is a feeling that institutions, political parties, universities, hospitals, security forces, schools, etc. are unfair, repressive and dismissive of certain minority groups. Dystopia as a fictional genre has settled in popular culture where zombies, technology-controlled societies, alien conspiracies, etc. are all common currency. Somehow, we appear to have arrived at the same conclusion as Rousseau did at the time of his writing.

The dominant factor in today's society, especially in political debates or the media, is not reason but feelings. This was exactly the case during the Romantic period. In our post-modern society, the important thing when establishing public policies is not reasoned arguments but the feelings of an impersonal general opinion. Social media is the vehicle to express that sentiment and many of the identity politics of our time go in this direction. It is enough to *feel* like a man or a woman to be one. It is enough to feel identified with a place or a language to proclaim the independence of a territory. It is enough to feel oppressed by some cause (justifiably or not) for it to be so. Rational arguments are not as powerful as the feelings to which they appeal and, more importantly, those feelings cannot be questioned.

The sociologist Zygmunt Bauman (1925–2017), who is mentioned above, speaks of 'liquid societies', that is, societies in which changes are so constant and rapid that they prevent institutions and customs from solidifying. The social fabric is

broken in a flow of individuals with weak relationships between them and their institutions. In his own words:

*The ground in which our life prospects are presumed to rest is
admittedly shaky -as are our jobs and the companies that offer
them, our partners and networks of friends, the standing we enjoy
in wider society and the self-esteem and-self confidence that come
with it. 'Progress', once the manifestation of radical optimism and
a promise of universally shared and lasting happiness, has moved
all the way to the opposite, dystopian and fatalistic pole of antic-
ipation: it now stands for the threat of a relentless and inescap-
able change that instead of auguring peace and respite portends
nothing but continuous crises and strain and forbids a moment of
rest. Progress has turned into a sort of endless and uninterrupted
game of musical chairs in which a moment of inattention results
in irrevocable exclusion. Instead of great expectations and sweet
dreams, 'progress' evokes an insomnia full of nightmares of being
'left behind' - of missing the train, or falling out of the window of
a fast-accelerating vehicle.*

In a post-modern society, the boundaries between the personal and the private, between men and women, between left
and right, between locals and foreigners, between humans and
animals, etc. are blurred. There are no clear barriers between
these opposites, and that causes us to re-evaluate many traditional roles in our society. A very significant part of the population, however, is reluctant to accept this new way of seeing
things. They prefer to cling to the past and that is one of the
main reasons why conflicts constantly emerge today within
our own societies.

This preference for how things were in the past is far from
being a reactionary and conservative right-wing attitude. Even

from a leftist political stance, the atomisation of society into identity groups (women, ethnic minorities, the gay community, retirees, religious minorities, nationalists, etc.) is seen as a failure of the traditional ideal of the left, which is 'unity and equality'.

Most of the criticism levelled against these groups does not affect the causes that they defend; however, what is really questioned is their combative and exclusive way of belonging to an identity group. This exclusive and belligerent attitude only makes an already dispersed society to be even more fragmented.

In fact, some analysts consider these movements as a sub-product of the capitalist system that, in theory, they intend to combat. The modus operandi is criticised because often the movements lose themselves in theatrical gestures and social media noise that critically detracts from their credibility. For instance, it is not uncommon to use famous people with a completely different life-style to support a certain cause unconnected to them. For example, Greenpeace has a list of famous people who contribute or make public awareness messages. Many of them are famous actors, pop or rock stars, models, athletes, etc. However, the customs and conspicuous consumption of many of them make it difficult for their lifestyle to be compatible with what they themselves preach. In addition, well-intended people set up superficial campaigns where reasoning is substituted by banal gestures or slogans. The luxury fashion designer Balenciaga has dedicated his fall-winter 2022 collection to the fight against climate change and the war in Ukraine. To do this, he has made the models parade down the catwalk in the middle of an artificial snowstorm. Unfortunately, this reduces the soundness of their demands that in many cases are fairly reasonable themselves.

Conclusion

There are certainly many countries in extreme difficulties at the present time. There are active wars in many parts of the world and we clearly do not live in a utopian society, but if today we were to answer the question posed by the Academy of Dijon in 1750[18], we would have numerous reasons to be optimistic.

Indicators of living standards have vastly improved (overall) in recent decades. Life expectancy, income and the access to hospitals or education have increased. Illiteracy, infant mortality and famines have all decreased. Diseases such as whooping cough, polio or diphtheria have been eradicated in practice. Besides, it is undeniable that scientific and technical development lies behind most of these advances.

In essence, we have as many arguments to be optimistic as we have to be pessimistic. It is a matter of feeling, not reason. However, it cannot be said that our feelings are completely arbitrary. On the contrary, they are highly conditioned by the information to which we are exposed. When that information is mostly negative, such as politicians insulting politicians, children harassed on social media, police beating protesters, racist attacks on athletes, natural disaster, etc., it is difficult to remain optimistic, despite many other advances in our societies. Needless to say, the solution is not to ignore these realities but to find a balance between catastrophism and total escapism.

In the present era of the so-called 'digital capitalism' it is expected that the users not only receive the news but also react

---

18. 'Have science and art really made us better individuals? And have they produced a fairer society?

to it. Perhaps this is because a higher number of interactions leads to more advertising revenue. The Canadian philosopher Marshall McLuhan (1911–1980) lived before the development of the internet, but he defined an analogous situation with the phrase: 'The medium is the message'. Undoubtedly, the way in which a message is conveyed influences the very interpretation of that message. That is why in today's media and social platforms, *culture wars* and controversies (sterile ones in many cases) are encouraged by both parties. They have economic value, but at the same time these discussions are not based on valid rational arguments. One cannot argue with feelings.

As it happened before with the Romanticism of the nineteenth century, these identity movements and the *cultural warriors* who support them, are half revolutionary and half reactionary. On the one hand, they are at the front line in defence of the rights of oppressed and marginalised groups. On the other hand, they also represent a new conservatism that dictates through its channels what is right or wrong. They punish those who do not agree with the substance of their ideas or criticise their methods. Whether we like them or not, these activists are probably as necessary as their critics, since this is the dialectical way in which history unfolds.

CHAPTER 10

NEW FORMS OF LOVE

'I hate, and I love.
How is that possible, you might ask.
I don't know,
but I feel that is the case,
and it haunts me.'

(Catullus)

Discussion

In our society, love is all around, literally. Dating apps are hugely popular but, do we still love and fall in love in the same way as we did in the past? Can we argue that the way we understand love and relationships is something different from what it used to be? Are we living a new sexual revolution or is it just the evolution (maybe a repetition) of certain patterns of behaviour? What do sciences, like psychology or neurology, have to say about love and how does it affect our perception of it? Is love the same thing as desire?

Introduction

Sappho is the name of a famous Greek poet who was born in the seventh century BC on the beautiful island of Lesbos. Very little in her biography can be taken for granted with the exception of her birthplace in Mytilene, the capital of Lesbos, and the fact that she founded a singing and dancing school for women. She called it '*House of the Muses' servants* and, depending on the source that we use, it was either a dissipated house of debauchery or a cultured and respectable place to educate girls in poetic arts, music and dance[19].

From her poems, it is not hard to deduce that she had several love affairs with some of the girls in the house (without forgetting that she also had relationships with men). It was not a word that existed during Sappho's life but with time, the love affair between two women was called 'lesbian love' precisely because Lesbos was her homeland.

Honestly, I wish I were dead.
Weeping many tears, she left me and said,
"Alas, how terribly we suffer, Sappho.
I really leave you against my will."

And I answered: "Farewell, go and remember me.
You know how we cared for you.

If not, I would remind you
...of our wonderful times.

---

19. Called the Tenth Muse by Plato, Sappho was a prolific poet of ancient Greece. She innovated the form of poetry through her first-person narration (instead of writing from the vantage point of the gods) and by refining the lyric meter.

For by my side you put on
many wreaths of roses
and garlands of flowers
around your soft neck.

And with precious and royal perfume
you anointed yourself.

On soft beds you satisfied your passion.

And there was no dance,
no holy place
from which we were absent."

(Sapphic fragments)

Unfortunately, only a tenth of her work has been preserved. In the year 1073, Pope Gregory VII ordered that all her poems had to be burned as they were considered to be immoral and full of sin.

In my eyes he matches the gods, that man who
sits there facing you—any man whatever—
listening from close by to the sweetness of your
voice as you talk, the

sweetness of your laughter: yes, that—I swear it—
sets the heart to shaking inside my breast, since
once I look at you for a moment, I can't
speak any longer,

but my tongue breaks down, and then all at once a
subtle fire races inside my skin, my

eyes can't see a thing and a whirring whistle
thrums at my hearing,

cold sweat covers me and a trembling takes
ahold of me all over: I'm greener than the
grass is and appear to myself to be little
short of dying.

(The Poetry of Sappho. Translated by Jim Powell)

Certainly, it would be unfair to reduce Sappho to her lesbian (or bisexual) condition. Her importance as a poet goes beyond that, her poems had an enormous influence on other classical authors. Even Plato, who by the way was not a great fan of poetry, considered her to be one of the muses.

Sappho with Erinna in the Garden of Mytilene (1864).

Among the many poets influenced by Sappho of Mytilene, there is one that stands out: Gaius Valerius Catullus (87–57 BC). This great Latin lyricist is best known for his love poems for his dear Clodia. They had a turbulent love story that was immortalised in the poet's work. Clodia was a married woman, and Catullus decided to hide her real name under a pseudonym. Since Clodia herself was also an admirer of the poet Sappho, Catullus decided to call her 'Lesbia'. It is under that name that she appears in some of the most beautiful love poems ever written in western literature.

However, Clodia did not fit the gender roles of the time. She was no angel. She conducted herself differently from how a good girl was supposed to behave and Catullus had never met a woman like her before. Although her husband was an important politician of the time, they were often seen arguing in public. It cannot be said that they had a happy marriage. When her husband died under strange circumstances, Clodia was under suspicion. During her husband's life she had affairs with several men. However, when Catullus started a relationship with Clodia, she was already a widow.

Although Catullus revered her in some of his poems, she was not always described in the most favourable terms. In a poem written as a lament to his friend, Caelius, he complained about her antics:

Caelius, our Lesbia, that Lesbia,
that Lesbia whom, alone, Catullus loved more than himself and
his own family,
now in the corners and in the alleys
she sucks off the descendants of the magnanimous Remo.

(Carmina LVIII)

Lesbia (John Reinhard Weguelin, 1878).

Interestingly, his friend Caelius also had an affair with Clodia, which ended even more dramatically. When he decided to break off their relationship, she accused him of trying to murder her by poisoning, and he was put on trial for it. Caelius's lawyer was the famous Latin orator Cicero (106–143 BC), and he certainly did a good job since the trial ended with the acquittal of Caelius. In Caelius's defence, Cicero painted a rather negative portrait of Clodia, accusing her of being a liar, a drinker, a gambler, as well as an incestuous and dissolute woman. It is difficult to know how Catullus felt about it and whether he was jealous or not, but it is still discussed today by philologists if the word 'jealous' is a variation of the name 'Caelius'.

There are two aspects that are interesting to mention in these love stories. The first one is the complexity and variety of affective and sexual relationships that existed in ancient times. Homosexuality, love triangles, open relationships, even paedophilia and incest were tolerated in some cases. Hopefully, this is enough to challenge our belief that the sexual practices of our time are extremely different from those of centuries ago. The common belief that in the past there was less sexual freedom.is not true. Sometimes the opposite was true.

In his poems dedicated to Lesbia (Clodia), the second relevant aspect is how Catullus depicts love from a new perspective. It is a more intimate and subtle feeling, full of contradictions and far from stereotypes. It is much closer to the idea of love that we have today. Precisely for this reason, Catullus' poems are still so relevant. This also means that love has not always been understood and expressed in the same way. The meaning of love, as the meaning of other big ideas such as truth, nature, culture or happiness, depends on the historical circumstances of the society we are considering. Since it has multiple interpretations, love is one of those ideas that is neither clear nor distinct but rather confusing and difficult to define.

We can approach the idea of love from a variety of disciplines, for instance: literature, philosophy or science. The examples are so abundant in the literary field that it would be easier to list the works that do not deal with love rather than those that do. However, the love described in those books is conceived and expressed in very different ways over time. *Romeo and Juliet* articulated an idea of love that might be acceptable for Shakespeare's society in the seventeenth century. Let's not forget that Juliet was 14 years of age. This idea of love is completely different from the love story of Apollo and Daphne in classical Greek mythology. Apollo was virtually forcing Daphne into carnal contact. He chased her blinded by desire as he was. Today, that would be the definition of rape or sexual harassment.

Lovestruck Apollo harassing Daphne. She preferred to become a tree rather than losing her virginity (Attributed to Piero del Pollaiuolo in the 15th Century).

Love in Plato's philosophy

In philosophy, love has been treated less than some other subjects. Ideas like 'freedom' 'life', 'happiness' or 'God' have been analysed more in detail. We can definitively find authors who dedicate a space to the idea of love in their work, but it usually occupies a secondary place. Among all the classic works that have been written on the subject, Plato's *The Symposium* remains an obligatory reference.

This dialogue between a group of friends who meet to eat, drink and chat, offers a conception of love and sexual relations that can shock even modern readers. Not only were sexual relationships between men tolerated, they were considered the perfect ones. The most exquisite love here, is not between a man and woman but between an adult man and an inexperienced young man who seeks in his lover something more than the enjoyment of the body or the pleasures of physical beauty. Plato does not specify the young man's age, but it certainly would not fit our current standards or, for that matter, our penal codes. And this is another example of how 'love' is conditioned by social and cultural factors. If these conditions change, our conception of what is acceptable and what is not in amatory matters also changes.

Plato believed that young lovers should dedicate themselves to seeking virtue, not carnal pleasure. One of the ways to become a better citizen was through a relationship with a virtuous older man. It would be the equivalent of today's 'mentoring'. For Plato, pleasing an older and honourable lover in order to obtain virtue is to love beautifully. The beloved young man must give himself to his older and virtuous lover because in this way the inexperienced youngster will benefit greatly. And not only that, the whole society wins because out of this relationship the young man will become a better citizen. When someone loves the body with the body, they love something transient and unstable. We all know that at some point a beautiful body will change and stop being beautiful. On the contrary, when a person's soul is loved, their object of love is stable and therefore preferable.

According to Platonic philosophy, the goal of love is immortality. There are two ways to achieve this goal: one is physical, in which men and women have sex in order to reproduce and continue this seemingly infinite process. This is an indirect and biological way of avoiding mortality by living through (the genes) of our descendants. The other way to achieve immortality is to love good and virtuous mature men because, from their union, a 'beautiful soul' will arise. In turn, this soul can, and must, reproduce again perpetuating the existence of good souls. This is the second and preferable way of securing immortality.

Considered in this light, these ideas might sound strange and senseless today, especially in a society in transition between modernity and post-modernity like ours. However, the moment we analyse them, we can see that these beliefs about soul mates and Platonic love remain very much alive today throughout popular culture: movies, musicals, soap operas, television shows, songs, poetry, etc. Maybe the language is a little different, but the essence of the message is the same.

One of the many examples that we can find in contemporary culture is the Spanish-Argentine film *Martín (Hache)* (1997). When one of the characters is asked if he prefers men to women, he replied:

'Minds seduce me. Intelligence seduces me. A face and a body seduce me when I see that there is a beautiful mind that moves

them and is worth knowing. Knowing, possessing, admiring...
I make love with minds. You have to fuck the minds.'

If we substitute the word 'mind' for the word 'soul', it could easily be considered a contemporary version of a platonic dialogue. In fact, the idea of platonic love as pure love, based on something that is not physical but intellectual in nature, has remained for posterity (albeit somewhat distorted as the relationship between older and younger males was not necessarily sexless). The influence of Plato's ideas on love has had a huge impact on Western culture and Christianity.

Courtly love

During the Middle Ages, a new literary movement arose and initiated a particular version of 'Platonic love'. Known as 'courtly love', it can be described as a rather aristocratic type of love (today we would say 'classist'). It was reserved for the upper classes of the Middle Ages as it was only the nobles (the ladies and gentlemen) who fell in love following the rules of courtly love. It was definitively not meant for the man and woman on the street. Those in charge of writing the rules of this new game were the troubadours who were themselves noble poets with a higher social and intellectual status. The minstrels, on the other hand, were destined to amuse the masses and the commons. Tania O'Donell in her *History of courtship* crudely expresses the difference:

Andre le Chapelain writing in the twelfth century, believed that the rules of love did not apply to farmers who he claimed resembled the beasts they cared for, by freely giving themselves up to lust as nature intended.

He counsels against allowing farmers the finer feelings in case this makes them too weak to fulfil their purpose of producing food for the community.

He also openly advises labourers to rape any lower class woman who takes their fancy, since her 'shyness' needs to be overcome. 'And if you should, by chance, fall in love with some of their women, be careful to puff them up with lots of praise and then, when you find a convenient place, do not hesitate to take what you seek and to embrace them by force'. Given that this advice is coming from a clergyman, one can see the open contempt that the nobility had for the peasantry. They were perceived as little more than animals to abuse and abandon.

On the one hand, courtly love was influenced by Christianity because, unlike in ancient Greece, same-sex relationships were no longer tolerated. On the other hand, it went against the Christian morals since it was a love that generally occurred outside of marriage. This is one of the main differences with the present time, because today, in our Western societies, marriage has to coincide with love. During the Middle Ages, love marriages were often the exception, not the norm. The other difference is that, for us, love is more democratic, not necessarily reserved for one particular class. Love is there for everyone to be consumed. Today, love is sometimes seen as a commodity, something commercial, not just a noble feeling (Valentine's Day, expensive rings, honeymoons, etc.).

The origin of courtly love is in the troubadours of the south of France, more specifically, in Provence. They developed this literary fiction with the intention of entertaining the ladies of the court in the twelfth century. During the crusades and the war campaigns in which knights were absent from their castles and palaces, boredom increased among the ladies. The troubadours' mission was to create and sing elaborate love stories to entertain them. The genre became so popular that it was the benchmark for good taste and distinction. Today, this role is fulfilled by soap operas, online pornography, Hollywood, Bollywood or certain reality TV programmes that are the reference in matters of lovemaking and romance.

Contrary to what it may seem, the love stories sung in the poems of the Middle Ages were not of adulterous passion. Many of their ideals were of renunciation, discipline, humiliation and servitude to the lady. Some of its characters had not even met their loved ones and, at times, the ladies did not even know about the existence of their admirers. Miguel de Cervantes (1547–1616) masterfully caricatured this in the relationship between Don Quixote and his dame Dulcinea. He fell in love with her without having seen her at all, not even once. He described her as a princess of blinding beauty when in reality she was a plain peasant.

Courtly love was considered a refined and elevated form of love, as opposed to vulgar or fleeting passion. From the books and verses of the poets, it passed to the halls of the castles. In the same way, the type of love and sex that is shown today on TV or mobile phones passed to the bedrooms of millennials and Z-gens.

From an educational point of view, courtly love also served a function. It taught the young men how to treat and respect the ladies. Women were not simple objects of desire; the gentlemen had to learn the rules of the waiting game, the gestures, the flirting glances, the right words… everything. The rhythm of restraint marked the steps to follow and, in many cases, love never culminated in physical contact or sex since they were mostly married women who preferred a Platonic love. Falling in love in the Middle Ages was a state of grace that elevated lovers above physical desire.

Sex, love and 'limerence'

As we have previously pointed out, courtly love has several elements in common with our current idea of romantic love. However, a differentiating element between the two is the role played by sex. Unlike what happened in the Middle Ages, in which ladies and knights could be in love without the slightest physical contact, today this would be difficult to understand[20]. Rather, the opposite could happen, since at the present time individuals can have numerous sexual relationships without being in love. This has coined new concepts such as "friend with benefits" (in post-modern terms: "fuck-buddies") or "open relationships". These were, until not so long ago, considered taboos.

Nowadays there seems to be a greater emphasis on sex. TV series, movies, songs, websites, etc. seem to corroborate it. In past times, renunciation, frugality and abstinence from carnal appetites were valued. In today's consumer society we could say that the opposite is happening. Consummation, possession and delight in sensual pleasures are celebrated (and many times shared on social media). Somehow, both love and sex have become commodified and transformed into something to be consumed.

---

20. This is not to say that in the Middle Ages there were no sexual relations between people of the same sex or before marriage.

The psychologist Dorothy Tennov (1928–2007) considered that our romantic idea of love evolved from a nine-
teenth-century idea that she calls 'limerence'. This term is a
neologism that refers to the state of infatuation suffered by
the lover. According to Tennov, the type of love that we constantly see in films, advertisements, literature, songs, etc., is in
reality a state of mind that includes obsessive thoughts about
the loved person. These feelings can only be directed towards
one individual exclusively. Frequently, this obsession is mixed
with fantasies and desires to form a relationship with the loved
one. Sexual consummation is not enough because the greatest
desire of someone in love is reciprocity. The feelings, fantasies
and obsessions need to be mutual as lovers constantly seek to
be corresponded in their feelings. It is not common, but it
can happen, that physical contact between lovers spoils the
feeling, although most of the time it has the opposite effect.

Traditionally, the most standardised version of a love story
with a 'happy ending' comes with the certainty that the feelings are reciprocated by the other person. We all know dramatic tales of unrequited love and how much pain it can cause
on the lover. Literature, in all its forms, is full of examples.

Today, when two people get married in Western countries
there is a public renunciation to any other romantic partner. In
the past that was not always the case as many marriages were
made out of convenience. They had to find love somewhere else.
The history of European monarchs is full of these examples.

New ways of loving?

According to the sociologist Zygmunt Bauman (1925–2017),
in today's society, the dominant attitude in amatorial affairs is

what he calls 'liquid love'. In his opinion, this is a shallow or superficial way of understanding relationships because there is no strong commitment or willingness to establish more meaningful connections. In our consumer societies, traditional romantic relationships are seen as limitations on individual freedom. Those affectional bonds are only worth maintaining until boredom sets in. When this happens, we can change partners in the same way we change a product in a store or a channel on TV. Much of the criticism directed at dating apps goes in this direction; that they seem to encourage this throwaway culture where users of these apps can go from one shallow relationship to another superficial one in perpetuity.

The divorce rate seems to supports Zygmunt Bauman's view of liquid love in our societies. Between 2017 and 2018, the percentage of divorces per marriages was 12% in Malta, 45% in the United States, 57% in Spain and 64% in Luxembourg. This increase can be interpreted in two different ways: either it is the realisation that love is not necessarily linked to marriage or that love and marriage are related, but as any other product in a consumer society, they have an expiration date. It is necessary to update our partners as the only way to perpetuate love, in the same way we update our phones.

Clearly, the data suggests that young people prefer to delay (or avoid) marriage. This, however, does not mean that they are celibate or reject the idea of having romantic relationships. Their main concern is that committing to a strong relationship will negatively affect their work-life, studies or leisure plans. It is also common to think that by having many experiences with different partners, the 'final choice' will be a better one, our soul mate (something that is very reminiscent of Plato). Consequently, the list of requirements for that hypothetical final partner is very long. In the perpetual search for the person who will make us complete and better individuals, we seek among other things: physical attraction, moral virtue, emotional and economic security, friendship, inspiration, tenderness, intimacy, care and good parental skills. Finding the person who meets all these criteria and getting them attracted to us is an ideal almost as unattainable as that of courtly love.

In reality, we are not looking for an individual but an ideal which is, again, something very Platonic. These high expectations often make the search unsuccessful and increase our frustration. The common complaint among individuals of a certain age group is that they feel the clock is ticking and they cannot find that partner who is supposed to complete them. It is perhaps for this reason that the prevailing idea about traditional relationships is seriously compromised. It is in this context where alternative forms of liaisons emerge. These are relationships that want to free themselves from the ideas commonly associated with romantic love. When this idea is broken down, the resulting variability is enormous. In philosophical terminology, we would say that the idea of love has been 'deconstructed' up to the point where some individuals marry themselves, or their pets, or even a tree.

Love and Science

From a scientific point of view, love has also been treated in different ways. Currently, the trend is to consider it from the brain functions of the person in love. They study and analyse the physiological effects on their bodies. The biologist Helen Fisher (1945) devoted herself for several years to the study of these questions. She observed that there are common traits in the individuals who are in love. The most common ones are:

- Feelings of euphoria.
- Insomnia or difficulty falling asleep.
- Loss of appetite.
- Excess energy.
- Greater ability to focus attention on a task.
- Tenacity in difficult situations.
- Consideration of the loved one as a new and unique being.

Many of these characteristics are not specific to humans as they can also be applied to most mammals and birds during the mating season. In consequence, this view lowers the status of love to a physiological function connected with a reproductive instinct, something that Plato called 'the desire for immortality'.

For her study, Helen Fisher had to find people who were 'madly in love' and willing to collaborate. She wanted to observe what is really happening in the brain of someone in love. After performing different scans on the volunteers who passed an initial test, she found that there were three chemicals involved in creating these feelings: dopamine, norepinephrine and serotonin. When the brain produces these three substances in certain proportions, the sensation we know as 'being in love' occurs.

But what makes us fall in love with some people and not with others? This is not a simple question, and therefore there is no simple answer, but it depends on some factors, such as gender or age. Men and women look for different things in their partners. Fisher believes that, generally speaking, we tend to have our sights on what is best for reproduction and rearing babies. The author is aware that her study is limited in its scope to love between men and women and avoids entering into other types of non-heterosexual romantic love.

According to her conclusion, the effects of love on the brain are always the same. It doesn't matter where or when because the results do not change. However, how we channel the feeling of being in love is largely determined by factors that are not chemical but cultural, such as the country, social class, level of education, economic status, etc.

Although it is far from being an original thought, another interesting idea pointed out by Helen Fisher is the fact that there are three different types of love:

1. Strong physical love that goes hand in hand with sexual desire. It is an urgent type of love, more basic and less elaborate in its forms.
2. Romantic love in the traditional sense. Here, courtship is more elaborated and there are many cultural factors that differentiate it between one society and another.
3. Gentle love, less sexual but related to care and affection. More connected with 'family love' and prolonged coexistence.

Romeo and Juliet (Frank Dicksee, 1884).

The chemicals involved in these types of love are also different, as well as the proportion in which they appear. In some cases, relationships go through all three phases, and other times they appear in only one of them.

It has been noted in clinical experiments the role of oxytocin in both love and desire, as it can have a different effect on both men and women. This could partly explain why women tend to look for relationships where there is a link between affection and desire. This is openly contested by many feminists who think that it is only a behavioural pattern that is learnt and not something that can be explained just using terms such as biology or nature.

From Helen Fisher's theories, we can deduce that falling in love is a state of intoxication in the brain produced by the combination of different chemical substances. Why only certain people trigger this reaction in us is still something less clear.

The evolution of love

As we have seen, 'love' can mean different things depending on the type of love we are talking about. Love has been expressed in different ways throughout history and depends on the society we are considering.

A key element in our society (especially during the period of infatuation) is kissing. In a multitude of novels, movies, TV series, etc., kissing is used as the definitive proof that the romantic interest is mutual and it is the climax of a great deal of fiction. However, some cultures do not have the habit of kissing as we know it. At least, they do not have the custom of putting their lips and tongues together. Kissing is definitely something that does not exist among chimpanzees or other primates. It is believed that human kissing may be a variation of passing chewed food from mouth to mouth, something that occurs between mothers and young chimpanzees. As this is a clear proof of caring and affection, it may be that kissing has become a symbol of affection between two people.

It is also very interesting that some societies are geographically very close but culturally they are very far away. Romantic relationships are still quite different around the world, even between bordering countries. For us, it is not strange that romantic love ends in marriage but in some Muslim countries, polygamy is a common institution and men can have multiple wives at the same time. In Western societies, however, the practice of polygamy contradicts the notion of romantic love. Conversely, in some areas of Tibet, polyandry still survives. A wife can have several husbands simultaneously, usually two men who are brothers, a practice that in the past was more widespread than it might seem.

Conclusion

By way of conclusion, we could say that although relationships in post-modern societies might seem very novel, they are only relatively original. It is also fair to conclude that these relationships will keep evolving in the future as conditions in each society change. However, science has shown us this century that there is something that is relatively stable: the chemical reactions in our brain when we are in love.

The ways in which love is manifested have varied throughout history, and our present age is no different. Currently, there may be new concepts related to love, such as 'polyamory' and some others, but a glance at classical mythology takes us back to a reality in which few things are really new.

What is probably different today is the number of relationships a person has throughout their life. As this number can refer to different types of relationships,.it makes generalisations about love and sexual relationships very difficult to sustain. The sentimental maps of a decade ago are useless today, and a compass to navigate through society is more essential than ever if we are to adapt ourselves to the changes in the territory.

CHAPTER 11

THE POLITICS OF THE BODY

'Where there is power,
there is resistance.'
(Michel Foucault)

Discussion

Who rules our bodies? Is it ourselves or is there a bio-power with access to the functions of our body? What are bio-politics? Why do we accept the authority of doctors, shamans, healers, virologists or gurus? And what happens when that authority is challenged? Does it make sense to question the legitimacy of vaccines? Should they be mandatory? Who has the power to decide such a thing?

Introduction

In the early 1940s, the Catholic Church introduced some changes to the liturgy. There were also some modifications in the way religion was taught until that moment. Catholicism is one of the most hierarchical religions in the world and the changes were introduced without too many problems among the priests and the faithful Catholic community. However, this was not the case in the Portuguese colony of Cape Verde, particularly on the island of Santiago, the largest and most populated of the archipelago.

In these Atlantic islands 900 km off the coast of Senegal, the practice of Catholicism had taken a turn that did not comply with the new demands of the Church. Among other things, some of the Cape Verdean priests were sexually very active, and they did not even try to hide it. They went as far as forming multiple families in the different islands of the colony as they were on evangelical missions.

To put an end to this and some other uncomfortable practices for the Catholic hierarchy, Portugal sent several priests in 1941 to replace the native religious leaders of these communities. On the island of Santiago, a minority rebelled against the imposition of the metropolis and they ended up fleeing to the mountains and other remote places with difficult access. There, they managed to continue with their traditions and practices, but at the same time, they created one of the most isolated communities in the planet as they decided to remain apart from the Church and the State (which at that time in Portugal were very close).

Members of this community were persecuted, detained and ridiculed for daring to challenge the dominant power at the time. As a consequence, they suffered many difficulties that

made them complete outcasts. This attitude, further complicated their already harsh living conditions, but despite everything, they remained faithful to their traditions and their
religious leaders.

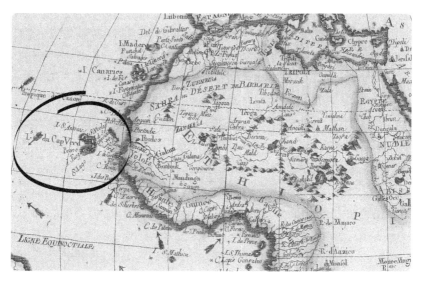

Old map of Africa with Cape Verde on the left.

Their protest was based on total disobedience, but always
in a peaceful manner. They never committed any act of vio-
lence. Instead, they refused to have any type of contact, direct
or indirect, with the State or the Church.

Their children were not attending school and in consequence they lacked any type of formal education. Several generations grew up not knowing how to read or write and none
of them was recorded in the civil registry. For practical purposes, they were not citizens like the rest of the Cape Verdean
population because they were not identified as such. In fact, it
was as if they did not exist at all. In an act of extreme rebellion,
they even refused to use proper names. Children were born in
the villages but they were not assigned a first name, in fact all
of them shared the name Rebels of Our Lord Jesus Christ.

In another step of complete opposition to a society that rejected and marginalised them, they decided not to use any public service, including hospitals. This was a risky move, but they refused vaccination for themselves or their animals.

This community was known as 'rabelados' (rebels) and on Saturdays and Sundays they travelled long distances on foot to be able to attend religious ceremonies organised by members of their society. On these days they also observed a full fast until past three in the afternoon.

With the passing of the time and the mediation of a social worker, the situation improved little by little. After the independence of the colony from Portugal in 1975, they began to gradually approach the society they had completely rejected in the past. However, it was a very slow transition since well into the 21st century, many of the *rabelados* still slept on the floor simply because they were lacking beds. They lived in houses made of cane and although they were a completely self-sufficient society, the living conditions were very harsh indeed.

Today, all children go to school and some of the few remaining *rabelados* sell paintings for tourists or have a morning job in the city so they can return to their communities in the afternoon. The old wounds have been finally closing and the population is blending with the world they once abandoned. Among the *rabelados* still remains a feeling of pride for belonging to a group that resisted, and peacefully fought against, the imposition of a political and religious power. Not only did they fight, they also managed to survive. That was a victory in itself.

The case of the *rabelados* of the island of Santiago is paradigmatic because they opposed the politics of the State and of the Catholic Church. Besides, they refused to be "biologically dictated" as they refused to go to hospitals, taking medicines or being vaccinated. Antonio Carlo Moniz of the University of Cape Verde describes the situation of the *rabelados* as follows:

"...this population group, living in areas of difficult access, excluded themselves from innovations, from school, from its teachings, from modern medicine and its practices, impregnated with strong religiosity (...). When necessary, they resorted to the traditional pharmacopoeia and quackery practices".

Relations of power

When Michel Foucault (1926-1984) analysed different relations of power, he realised that power does not only exist in governments or between kings and subjects. Power is everywhere. The relationship between teachers and students, parents and children or doctors and patients are also relationships of power where there is an authority that exercises power over a subject who obeys. The source of authority in this hierarchy comes from a certain type of superior knowledge that justifies the whole situation. This superior knowledge can be of various types such as medicine, science, experience, religious dogmas, etc.

These hierarchical power relations are not good or bad in themselves. Some of the results have been very positive and, as we all know, many others have not. If we consider the particular case of medicine, there is a type of authority that tries to regulate and control the biological functioning of the subjects - our bodies - hence the name 'bio-politics'. Doctors, scientists, academics and so on, are in charge of telling us what is good or bad. We attribute to them the authority to control many things in our lives: our diet, our access to work, our sexual practices, the chemical balance of our brain or even our physical movement. All this because they have direct access to some superior knowledge that we lack.

Obviously, the *rabelados* had no idea about Foucault or bio-politics, but with their attitude they actually opposed this practice by renouncing access to hospitals, education, modern medicine and vaccines. They are still admired for it by some groups.

Many of those who opposed being vaccinated against Covid-19 were invoking a similar right to that of the *rabelados*. They claimed to be fighting against the imposition of a dominant power over their bodies and therefore they resisted being vaccinated. It was an act of resistance, a defence of their individual freedom. As a consequence, they opened an interesting debate: what are the limits of a state or any other institution such as health authorities? Is it acceptable to force vaccination among those who do not want to? Do these individuals have the right to decide freely even at the risk of their own health and the health of others? Can we tolerate political games just by invoking a greater good?

In the case of the *rabelados*, they were rejecting modern medicine not because they were anarchist or radical freedom fighters but simply because they were under the influence of a different kind of authority. In this case they chose to obey the authority of their religious leaders and traditional healers.

In Western countries, on the other hand, scientific and medical knowledge has been considered as an acceptable source of bio-political power. We accept the regulation of our bodies through the practices that modern medicine impose on us: hospitals, doctors, surgeons, psychologists, etc. This power is legitimised on the basis that they have access to a superior type of knowledge about what is best for our bodies and our lives. The *rabelados* did the same thing, although their source of authority was very different and their public health practices were also very archaic.

Many of those who rejected Covid-19 vaccines had an attitude of rebellion against scientific and medical authorities. They were not ready to accept that such authorities can regulate their bodies simply because they are repositories of superior knowledge: medical science, in this case.

This attitude of opposing a bio-power is not something new, as we have seen in the case of the *rabelados*. Foucault's maxim is still valid: 'Where there is power, there is resistance'.

Covid vaccines were also rejected among some members of Islamic communities because of a rumour that traces of pork were among the components of the vaccines, and this would contradict their religious practices.

What is more novel and characteristic of post-modern societies is the multiplicity of alternative authorities that could be used to oppose medical science. With the *rabelados* there was only one possibility because traditional medicine and its religious practices were more important. However, with today's 'anti-vaxxers' it does not seem so obvious. There is a large part of the population that attributes the same (or higher) authority to alternative medicines like acupuncture, chiropractic, homeopathy, naturopathy or Ayurvedic medicine. Sometimes, this belief in alternative medicine stems from religious or metaphysical ideas, but sometimes is a criticism of the excessive medication and vaccination imposed by Western medicine. Although it might seem surprising, a significant number of people believed that some powerful governments inserted a chip into our bodies when we were administered Covid vaccines. They think that there is an elite that controls our biological data so we can be easily manipulated.

Smallpox, cows and 'antivaxxers'

For centuries, smallpox was a deadly disease that was also highly contagious. It ended the lives of millions of people and even those who survived had to live with the consequences. Visible marks and scars were a sign of having suffered from a disease which, in some cases, even resulted in blindness.

Between fever, vomiting, sores and skin rashes, the sick could agonize for weeks. Its contagious capacity did not help in the caring of the sufferers either. Smallpox has undoubtedly been one of the greatest causes of death among human beings in history.

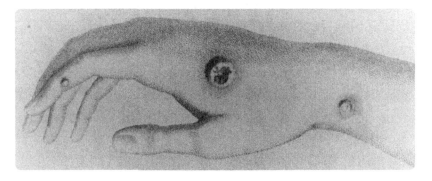

Effects of smallpox on human skin.

Fortunately, the last diagnosed case of smallpox dates back to 1977. But how did it go from being the cause of death of 300 million people in the 20th century to being almost completely eradicated as a disease? The answer lies largely in cows (and the word for 'cow' in Latin is 'vacca' and hence the name 'vaccines').

It had been observed that people who were in direct contact with cows and horses (such as farmers and cavalrymen, for example) did not develop the disease, or at least not to the same extent.

To protect his family, the farmer Benjamin Jetsy (1736-1816) decided to inoculate his wife and his children with the cowpox virus. Although extremely risky, the experiment worked well and everyone developed immunity to human smallpox, a much more deadly variant. About 22 years later, in 1796, the British citizen Edward Jenner scientifically disclosed the discovery and so vaccines were born.

However, from the very first moment, there were critics and sceptics challenging the results. In addition, there was great concern about possible side effects of the vaccines. Some people considered it an aberration to be inoculated with a virus that came from a cow. It was just not a Christian thing to do. God certainly would not have wanted us to mix with animals in this way. Others considered that inoculation with animal substances would produce humans with cow features. Perhaps they would grow horns or give rise to mutants like minotaurs.

The Wonderful Effects of the New Inoculation! (James Gillrae, 1802). Cartoon showing the perverse effects of vaccines.

In the 19th century, people started to form anti-vaccine leagues as they considered the requirement to be vaccinated a limitation of their freedom. It is a neat example of citizens resisting what they perceived as an interference of the State in the way we govern our bodies. Their logic then, as it is today, goes as follows: *In my body, I decide. It is my right to choose what I take or reject. My body is my temple.*

Many citizens of some countries are suspicious of health institutions. They distrust the intentions of the State and of the big pharmaceutical companies. Many also doubt the convenience of vaccines because their possible side effects have not yet been sufficiently studied. In the case of Covid-19, they feel that the usual testing process has been rushed. In some cases, this might be true.

Throughout the history of medicine we can easily find numerous examples of treatments and remedies that caused more problems than they solved. Thalidomide was synthesized in 1953 by Wilhem Kinz and, thanks to its properties, was considered a good remedy to treat nausea and dizziness in pregnant women. Its use quickly spread to numerous countries and it was not until 1961 that it was connected to the malformation of foetuses during pregnancy. It is estimated that more than 10,000 babies were born with severe deformities during the drug's marketing period.

Armed with arguments like this, 'anti-vaxxers' have posed some interesting questions. To what extent does the State have the right to force its citizens to be vaccinated? Some countries made vaccination against Covid-19 compulsory and others severely limited the number of activities for the unvaccinated. Can we say that it is a bio-political form of blackmail for everyone to accept the vaccines? Are the so called 'liberal states' acting like totalitarian ones? Are individual liberties and public health really in conflict? Should young people under 18 and children also be vaccinated? These are all relevant issues for a good philosophical debate. However, action had to be taken before there was a general consensus on the suitability of mass vaccination. The ruling powers had found themselves in a situation that generated friction among those with an alternative view.

Other forms of control

Vaccines, or medical science in general, is just one of the many different instruments that bio-politics use, but there are others. A recent example is the demographic control that the People's Republic of China has carried out from 1979 until 2015. Parents who had more than one child would had to pay fines and they are directly responsible to cover the cost of any health service. The original goal of the measure was to curb population growth, but judging by the negative results in society, it is doubtful it could be counted a success. It generated other unintended consequences as it was the beginning of a sad practice in which couples opted for selective abortions in favour of male babies. Men were considered to be more valuable in agricultural work and women more of a liability. The number of young males became so disproportionate in some parts of the country that in turn caused other problems such as the lack of female partners to form a family. Again, the Chinese government intervened to prohibit doctors from revealing the sex of foetuses before birth under very severe penalties. Hospitals were not allowed to make this type of diagnosis in the hope to restore the lost balance.

In another example of bio-politics on a large scale we should mention eugenics. It was an attempt to apply Darwinism to humans in society. The Victorian polymath scientist Francis Galton in the nineteenth century defined it as a system that would allow 'more suitable races or strains of blood a better chance of prevailing speedily over the less suitable'[21]. For decades, eugenics was considered a science in many universities and it was taught as an academic discipline that students needed to study in its principles. It was not until well into the twentieth century that it began to be questioned. Nazi Germany carried out a secret program with the clear objective of eradicating individuals who had been born with what they considered to be some type of physical or mental deficiency. To give an idea of the scientific nature of the principles, it suffices to say that there was a category which also included homosexuals. It is estimated that some 300,000 individuals were eliminated in psychiatric hospitals under the justification of "racial hygiene" and economic reasons. They were considered social parasites that imposed a financial burden on the state. Nazi society aspired to be culturally and physically superior and it was morally justified to get rid of the elements that might make the population weaker.

At the time, some German doctors had the authority to select 'incurably ill' patients and give them a 'merciful death'. In the case of children, this meant letting them starve, although at other times they were given barbiturates along with their meals. Others were simply injected with morphine and scopolamine. When it came to adults these methods were considered too slow and so it was decided that an acceptable alternative was to gas them with carbon dioxide. In order for

---

21. He was knighted in 1909.

the 'patients' to enter the chambers without resistance, the walls were covered with tiles and thus the rooms gave the impression of being a shower. Without suspecting what would happen next, the so-called patients voluntarily entered naked. Death occurred in just a matter of minutes. It was precisely that brutal efficiency that greatly pleased the authorities responsible for the programme.

Gas chamber designed to look like a shower.

Mass vaccination, the prohibition of abortion, birth control and eugenics are all bio-political practices in which a power regulates the behaviour of individual bodies. However, as we have seen in all these different examples, some can have very positive results (such as the eradication of smallpox) and others are truly atrocious (such as the extermination of individuals who were considered inferior).

Conclusion

A growing tendency in post-modern societies is to be wary of any bio-political power. The truth is that if we look at some of the examples we have considered earlier in this chapter, there are plenty of reasons for that. However, if we are guided by the idea that 'our body is our temple' and that any bio-political practice has to be previously approved by every single individual, then it is inevitable that conflicts will arise. Likewise, many public health policies will be controversial too. If we are the final judges of what happens in our body, there will be situations in which there is a conflict of interest between the general good of the majority and that of the individuals.

To illustrate this situation, some young antivaxxers declared that they did not want to live in a gerontocratic regime where the elderly, with their demanding public health needs, impose what the younger (and the healthier) have to do with their bodies.

It is obvious that not the entire adult population needs to be vaccinated against Covid-19, but the alternative of not doing so could have created even worse consequences. It might be argued that mass vaccination of the adult population has been the least bad option at a moment in time when quick decisions had to be made. The subtle and detailed debate (although very interesting and necessary) was not the priority when the lives of many people were in danger.

It is from the 60s and 70s with the post-modern philosophy of Michael Foucault that numerous alternatives (and protests) begin to appear. They go against the decisions of the political and bio-political powers. It is in this light that we should understand today's debate on vaccines in particular and the questioning of authorities and experts in general.

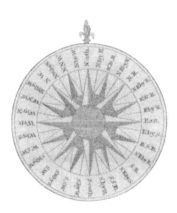

CHAPTER 12

DEATH: THE GRAND FINALE

Can I die?

(Jacques Derrida)

Discussion

What does death mean to a post-modern society? Is it a clear and distinct concept or, on the contrary, are there different ways of approaching the subject? Are all living things biologically doomed to age and die? Is death a singular event or rather a process? The mind/body dualism plays a very important role but how does it affect our ideas of life and death? How has the idea of death evolved throughout history? What does contemporary philosophy have to say about it? What is the 'future' of death? Can we escape, (albeit partially) from death? And, as it is rhetorically asked in post-modern philosophy, is my own death possible?

Introduction

When Perenelle married Nicolas de Flamel in 1368, he would be her third and last husband. Also, he became the most notorious of the three.

At 48 years old, she would no longer have any more children, despite the fact that he was much younger than her. However, the couple did not need any descendants to perpetuate their long-lasting legacy after their death. Or perhaps we should say the opposite, that they actually became famous for never having died.

Perenelle brought a substantial dowry to her new marriage and her husband was himself a wealthy-enough bookseller who owned two shops in Paris. Together, they came to be great benefactors of pious and religious works, as well as contributors to the construction of several churches. No one would question that they were devout Catholics. However, this did not prevent them from having an interest in a discipline that many considered heretical, a practice that the Catholic Church itself would later denounce: alchemy.

Alchemical symbology.

Despite this fame, it was not until the 17th century that Nicolas and Perenelle were considered the great alchemical figures that they are today. Legend has it that Nicolas had a premonitory dream in which an angel showed him a book with some images. This angel spoke to him directly and assured him that he would be the only one to decipher what they meant. Shortly after having the dream he was walking through a market when stranger approached to him with an ancient book. It was written in a language he did not recognise and it contained very suggestive images. It was authored by Abraham the Jew[22] and it seemed to describe the process of obtaining the greatest prize any alchemist could imagine: the philosopher's stone. This enigmatic object had the double property of turning metals into gold but it was also the main ingredient for the elixir of eternal life. The person who drunk a small amount of its powder dissolved in water would be cured of all diseases and ailments. Not only that, this person would also live forever. Humans would become like gods; they would have eternal life. The philosopher's stone could make anyone's dream come true: wealth, health and immortality. However, being in possession of a secret like this conferred great power, so anyone working on this matter would normally do so in secrecy.

For 21 years, Nicolas Flamel tried to decipher the contents of the book; it became his life's task. Lacking answers, he traveled to Santiago de Compostela (Spain) on pilgrimage and took with him some pages of the book. On the way back to Paris he met the enigmatic Maestro Canches in León. He was a Spanish Jew converted to Christianity and crucially, someone who could understand the content of the book, helping Nico-

---

22. Little is known about the life of this German Jew, who was an alchemist, magician, and philosopher, born in 1362.

las in his endeavour. With the intention of showing him the complete book, Flamel convinced Canches to accompany him to Paris. However, he fell ill during the trip and died. Luckily, with what he had learnt from Canches and three more years of study, Nicolas Flamel managed to translate the entire book and decipher the secrets contained therein.

In turn, Nicolas Flamel taught his wife Perenelle the principles of alchemy and together they began preparations for the philosopher's stone. Initially, they were not that successful but it is said that they managed to transform metals into silver. With more practice and time, they perfected the technique and succeeded in producing gold.

Nicolas and Perenelle also drank from the elixir of life and therefore they became immortal. In fact, during the 17th and 18th centuries, some authors claimed to have seen Nicolas Flamel at a time when he should have been dead centuries ago. They tried to explain this apparent contradiction by saying that after drinking from the elixir Nicolas and Perenelle faked their own deaths. This is the reason why people from different eras claimed to have come into contact with them. In literature they are recurring characters, such as in Victor Hugo's novel *The Hunchback of Notre Dame* or in *Harry Potter and the Philosopher's Stone*. According to legend, they are still alive today and they would be close to 700 years old.

The story of Nicolas Flamel shows how the search for eternal life seems to be a constant in human history. In this view, death is a limitation, a punishment and a curse. Stubbornly, human beings do not seem able to resign to its inevitability; they are always trying to find a way to escape death. However, maybe we should not be so assertive in claiming that the flight from death is a constant in all living beings. Perhaps we should learn about Pelle's story first. After all, some people actively search for death in life as a form of liberation.

Per Yngve Ohlin was known as 'Pelle' by his family and friends. He was born in Sweden in 1969 not far from the capital Stockholm. Unfortunately, he was not very popular at school and was bullied by some of the kids. He occasionally received beatings and in one of them his spleen was ruptured causing internal bleeding. The incident was so serious that for a short period of time the doctors considered him clinically dead. Luckily, they managed to stabilise him at the hospital and he made a full recovery. Pelle never revealed the truth of what had happened and, if he was asked about the episode, would normally reply that he had an accident while skating. It was his brother who many years later explained what really happened.

Per Yngve Ohlin (Pele), aso known as 'Dead'.

Possibly, as a result of this traumatic experience, Pelle developed a morbid interest in death and all things related to funeral symbols and rites. Musically, he was very interested in heavy metal groups and wanted to be part of a band with similar tastes. After forming a group that didn't work out in his native Sweden, he decided to get in touch with *Mayhem*, a Norwegian band that was looking for a vocalist. Pelle sent them a package containing a letter, a cassette, and a crucified mouse. With that gesture he definitively caught the attention of the band. It wasn't long until he moved to Norway and by 1988 was already a member of the band.

It was customary for black metal[23] members to have a stage name and Pelle decided to call himself 'Dead' because in reality, as he explained, he was not human, he was a creature from a different world. He had visions and he thought that the blood in his veins was frozen and he was not really alive.

Today we know that Pelle most likely suffered from a rare mental condition known as Cotard's syndrome in which people tend to believe that they are dead, have no blood, lack internal organs or are in a state of putrefaction. Strangely enough, many of those who suffer from this syndrome also believe that they are immortal.

Pelle also suffered periods of deep depression and he was constantly self-harming. He was attracted to everything that was directly or indirectly related to death. He used white make-up to look like a corpse, self-mutilated, slept with dead animals under his bed, and buried his clothes in the ground for several days to acquire that quality of 'dead clothes'. His behaviour at concerts contrasted with his attitude in daily life, deeply reserved, melancholic and withdrawn. Before going on

---

23. The early Norwegian black metal scene of the 1990s is credited with creating the modern black metal genre and produced some of the most acclaimed and influential artists in extreme metal. It attracted massive media attention when it was revealed that its members had been responsible for two murders, a suicide, and a wave of church burnings in Norway.

stage he inhaled a bag in which he kept dead animals, He wanted to have the 'perfume of death' while he was performing. Sometimes, he would cut himself in public and throw pig heads and blood into the crowd. Although it was not to everyone's liking, it gave the group some notoriety and attracted the attention of some people looking for more extreme experiences.

It was this attention that greatly pleased Euronymous, the band's guitarist. Despite the fact that his relationship with Pelle was not very good (they already had several fights and on one occasion Pelle stabbed him with a knife) Euronymous thought that this chaotic and dangerous image benefited the group. They were becoming a group with the ability to shock the Norwegian society. They were also connected to the wave of church arsons in the country.

Pelle was convinced that he did not belong in this world and he was constantly looking for a way out. On April 8, 1991 he did exactly what he said, as described in his farewell note:

Excuse the blood, but I have slit my wrists and neck. It was the intention that I would die in the woods so that it would take a few days before I was possibly found. I belong in the woods and have always done so. No one will understand the reason for this anyway. To give some semblance of an explanation I'm not human, this is just a dream and soon I will wake. It was too cold and the blood kept clotting, plus my new knife is too dull. If I don't succeed dying to the knife I will blow all the shit out of my skull. Yet, I do not know. I left all my lyrics by "Let the good times roll"—plus the rest of the money. Whoever finds it gets the fucking thing. As a last salutation may I present 'Life Eternal'. Do whatever you want with the fucking thing. / Pelle. I didn't come up with this now, but seventeen years ago.

Unfortunately, it was Euronymous who found Pelle's life-less body. What he did next left everyone stunned and shows his real character. Instead of seeking help or calling the police, he went out to buy a camera and photographed the scene. He even moved some objects to make everything more 'artistic'. He put the knife and the gun next to Pelle's body. He claimed that his intention was to carry out an artistic project and he had the time to make a necklace with the remains of the skull. He phoned another member of the band and told him that Pelle had done "a really cool thing", he had killed himself. Shockingly, in an album released in 1993 he used one of the photos of the suicide on the cover, and with that action he gained the hate of a large part of the black metal world. Euronymous made several enemies himself and ironically, he was killed a couple of years later by another musician he had previously collaborated with. The Norwegian metal scene of the time was no joke at all.

The problem

It is clear that for most people death is not a popular topic in a conversation. Except in certain contexts it is a taboo subject, even more so than sex, money or politics. This causes confusion and obscures any attempt to understand what it means for us today.

Death, like the idea of love, can be approached from different disciplines: science, philosophy, anthropology, religion, history, etc. None of these disciplines exhausts the idea of death. It is also interesting to see how often these disciplines clash with each other to the point that sometimes they do not even refer to the same thing.

From a biological perspective, death seems to be an inevitability for all living organisms. Life is the opposite of death and every living organism perishes sooner or later. However, we now know that there are some organisms, such as the jellyfish Turritopsis dohrmii (Immortal Jellyfish) that seem to have developed a kind of biological immortality. Unlike other living organisms, their cells do not age or degrade, they are free from the process of senescence (the gradual deterioration of functional characteristics in living organisms).

This means that their cellular activity does not deteriorate and they are able to maintain their biological functions unchanged indefinitely. Only through an external destruction process (for example being eaten by another individual) can they die.

These types of organisms seem to be the exception as almost all living beings reach a limit and die. The cells that make up the body stop fulfilling the biological functions that are necessary for the maintenance of life. This is what we commonly describe as 'death by natural causes' or 'dying of old age'.

Some types of jellyfish are biologically immortal with no maximum lifespan.

One of the big changes in our current conception of death is that we no longer perceive it to be an event that occurs at a certain moment (for instance, on a certain day and hour). In reality, death is a constant process of deterioration of cellular activity and that process can last for many years. Put in a much more dramatic and literary way: there comes a point when living is dying one day at a time. However dramatic it might sound, it should not be viewed from a tragically pessimistic perspective as many of these deteriorating processes are also reversible. Luckily for many of us, there is one branch of regenerative medicine that goes in this direction.

It would appear that for medicine death is a clear enough state that does not generate any controversy. However, it is shocking that there is no consensus between some hospitals and certain medical specialties (for example, between neurology and cardiology) on what constitutes 'death'. For some, it is the permanent cessation of electrical brain functions. For others, it occurs only when there is cardiac arrest and loss of breathing and pulse, although this has been contested since the systematic application of CPR. Many patients have been resuscitated after spending a considerable time without a pulse or breathing.

Although this lack of medical consensus may seem like a minor issue, the problem of defining death has consequences in other areas, such as if the person is an organ donor. It also generates conflict in legal cases related to death certificates, medical bills, life insurance or inheritance.

In this sense, it should be noted that biological death is not the same as legal death. For biological death to be certified, a body must exist; however, in cases of accidents or disappearances under suspicious circumstances, only legal death can be certified, but not biological death. In some countries, it takes several years for a missing person to be declared legally dead.

Death through history

It is currently estimated that 150,000 people die worldwide every day. If we do a rough calculation, that means a million deaths in a week, 4.5 million in a month or 54 million in a year. It is as if the entire population of Italy disappeared in little more than a year.

Despite being such a frequent phenomenon, today we have distanced ourselves from direct contact with death in the same way that we have distanced ourselves from the origin of our food (plantations, orchards, farms, slaughterhouses, etc.). In developed countries, two-thirds of deaths occur in hospitals. People no longer die at home surrounded by family and friends with the spiritual company of a priest, as was the case in the past. Some authors refer to this phenomenon as 'invisible death'. In post-modern societies there is little direct contact with death, or with dead bodies. Our exposure to it is usually symbolic or indirect, for example through art or television shows about true crime, hospitals or autopsies.

Sheet from the 'Book of the Dead'.

Although biological death is a universal fact that sooner or later all human beings will encounter, in reality people do not

always die in the same way. This means that there is a historical and cultural element associated with biological death. We
are not talking about the causes of death, which in many cases
are also historical, cultural and very permeable to factors such
as diet, education, social class, economic status, etc. What we
are trying to say here is that there is a historical and cultural component in our conception of death. Whatever death
means to us, and what implications it entails, it is something
that goes far beyond the biological realm and connects directly with philosophy, religion, ethics, economics, politics, etc.

Like many other ideas such as freedom, love, nature, culture, God, matter, etc. there is a shift between pre-modern,
modern and the post-modern conception.

In pre-modern times, the dominant idea is that of death
as the end of material life and the beginning of a spiritual
one. The body dies but not the soul, which is immortal and
independent. In ancient Egypt, the pharaohs were buried with
papyri with instructions for when they arrived in the afterlife.
These scrolls contained incantations, advice and spells in order
to avoid the many dangers of the afterworld. They also provided help in finding a life without sadness, pain or anger. It was
the so-called 'Book of the Dead', a travel guide to the afterlife.

It is impossible to exaggerate the importance of Plato in the
philosophy and religion of the West. In several of his works
he describes how the soul, unlike the body, is immortal. Once
the body perishes, the soul leaves it. Plato also mentions that
the actions that one has chosen during one's life have consequences after death. The souls of those who have been righ-
teous ascend to heaven and those who have been unrighteous
descend to the bottom of the earth. As we can see, this is the
same idea that five centuries later Christianity took up again,
and persists even today.

For Plato the soul gives life to the body and since the soul is immortal, death is only the end of material life. Once the body is dead, the soul will look for another body to give life to. Souls are neither created nor destroyed, their total number is limited and constant. When someone is born, it does not mean that a new soul is born, but rather that the soul comes from a body that has previously died and enters the newborn.

The importance of the soul over the body is taken to the extreme when Christianity considers the pleasures of the body to be sinful and glorifies renunciations in favour of a pure soul. For Christians, once the body is dead, the soul will live eternally in the glory of God only if this soul has been pure, but it will suffer in hell if it has been carried away by the appetites of the body.

During the process of transition (which we call the Renaissance) between pre-modern society and modern society, we see the development of a scientific mentality that begins to eliminate some of the mythological explanations of the previous era. However, that does not mean that these types of myths disappeared. In fact some of them remain among us even today.

Materialism and rationalism reduce the explanatory capacity of myths. There is a gradual change from myth to science (although some post-modern authors say that religious myths are actually replaced by scientific myths). Motivated by this new scientific and rational attitude, modern thinkers begin to question whether there is life after death. The possibility of a life disconnected from corporeal matter is gradually doubted by modern thinkers.

Although it has been said on numerous occasions that rational and scientific thought leads to the liberation from religious beliefs and the will of gods, what is often forgotten is that it also eliminates the comforting belief that after this material life there is another spiritual one awaiting us. It is some kind of undefined place in which consciousness would continue to exist, but without the body. With the loss of this 'safety net' some pessimistic philosophers started to see life as meaningless, full of suffering and without reward for those who had been good, or as punishment for those who had been evil. Arthur Shopenhauer (1788-1869) believed that human life was so insignificant and petty, so sterile and meaningless, that we would not endure immortality and in the end we would voluntarily ask for death. In his view, 'absolute death' became a moral necessity.

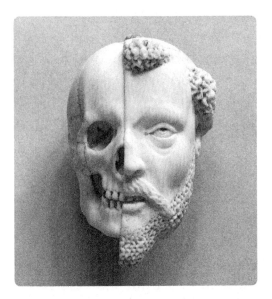

French 16th/17th-century ivory pendant, Monk and Death, recalling mortality and the certainty of death.

Other authors go in the opposite direction and make an ode to life. They invite us to get the most out of it without worrying too much about death. Friedich Nietzsche (1844-1900), although initially a disciple of Shopenhauer, described life as taking place in a finite material universe, and therefore it could be that our life repeats itself over and over again as an eternal return. Would we want to be eternally worried about death or ,on the contrary, fully enjoy life? Nietzsche exchanged the eternity of death for the eternity of life (albeit theoretically, as constant repetition).

However, a scientific mindset does not exclude the belief in an afterlife. In the 20th and 21st centuries there are many examples of religious scientists who believe that after our biological death there will be some other kind of life. In post-modern societies, a large part of the population has gone from a belief in life after death with a religious connotation to a more secular belief in life after death. Instead, the religiosity has been substituted for pseudo-scientific terms like energy, magic, independence of consciousness from the body, etc. In fact, it is very complicated, even for the most rational and scientific atheist mentality, to think that after this material life there isn't another one waiting for us. Sigmund Freud (1856-1939) famously said that in the unconscious of each person there is a certainty of immortality:

No one believes in their own death. Or to put the same thing another way: in the unconscious, every one of us is convinced of our own immortality.

The 20th century and beyond

In academic circles there are disputes about who was the most important philosopher of the 20th century. Generally, in the English-speaking world, that merit falls to the Austrian Ludwig Wittgenstein (1889-1951). His main focus of study was language from a logical and rational perspective. However, about death he wrote:

Death is not an event in life: we do not live to experience death. If we take eternity to mean not infinite temporal duration but timelessness, the eternal life belongs to those who live in the present. Our life has no end in the way in which our visual field has no limits.

This idea of death is very similar to that of Epicurus (341 BC-270 BC) in ancient Greece when he wrote that:

Death is nothing to us. When we exist, death is not; and when death exists, we are not. All sensation and consciousness ends with death and therefore in death there is neither pleasure nor pain. The fear of death arises from the belief that in death, there is awareness.

The other philosopher who competes to be the most influential of the last century is Martin Heidegger (1889-1976). He is much more appreciated in continental Europe, Japan and Latin America than in the Anglo-Saxon sphere (and by the way, the distinction between continental and British philosophy has a long tradition of several centuries). For some academics Heidegger is nothing more than a charlatan who had no regard for accuracy or precision. Nor was he a writer who had much empathy with his readers as his texts are notoriously difficult to understand. Part of this difficulty arises from his idea that it was necessary to create a new language. He thought that he was talking about something different that had not been studied before in Western philosophy. He wanted to change the direction of Philosophy and to do that he used an obscure language with many invented terms and neologisms.

The Anglo-Saxon philosophy, on the other hand, prefers clarity and rigour (sometimes to the extreme) in the use of language. This, together with the fact that Heidegger was a member of the German Nazi party, make him a controversial figure. Academics are divided between those who do not separate Heidegger's life from his work and those who do. Regardless of what we think of him, the truth is that Heidegger's influence on 20th century philosophy is enormous, especially on existentialism and on the so-called post-modern philosophers. It is for this reason that he is a very relevant figure on this topic.

The interest of Heidegger's philosophy here lies in the centrality that death has in human existence. He defined individuals as 'beings for death' meaning that what is most typical of the human being is mortality. This is the feature that defines us and the most absolute certainty of our existence; one that should be the principle that governs everything else and the guide to a full life. It might sound paradoxical, but death is what makes life worth it. It is not possible to live fully, or as Heidegger would say, 'authentically' ignoring death. We need to come to terms with the idea of making death part of our vital project. In this sense, Heidegger's opinion went against Freud, Wittgenstein and Epicurus. In Heidegger, death is the limit of everything, and consequently our life plan is conditioned by this limited duration. Death gives meaning to existence because existence by itself is not a totality. Totality is achieved with death, or rather, between the union of existence and death in a vital project.

In the existentialist philosophy of Jean Paul Sartre (1905-1980) death also plays a crucial role, but unlike Heidegger, he believed that death simply showed the absurdity of life. Death was not the conclusion to anything; it was only the unwanted and undesirable interruption of human freedom. For Sartre, the human being was a 'useless passion'. Sartre seemed to be saying that on the one hand we wish for immortality but in reality we are just futile, contingent and mortal. We would like to be God but we are only human. This unfulfilled longing necessarily generates frustration and vital anguish. The way this feeling manifests itself is described admirably well by Woody Allen. He compares this feeling to a person who normally gets up every morning at 8am, but one day has to catch a plane and needs to get up at 6am. During that night, the person cannot rest well thinking that maybe he will fall asleep and miss the flight. This is the anxiety of life regarding death in Sartre's existentialism. And Woody Allen ends his autobiography with another witty thought about death:

'Whatever happens to my work when I'm gone is totally irrelevant to me. After death, I suspect very little will get on my nerves (...) Rather than live on the hearts and mind of the public I prefer to live on in my apartment.'

In a particularly twisted way, Heidegger described death as the possibility of absolute impossibility. When we are alive we have many possibilities but when we are dead, everything is impossible. However, we know that the impossibility that death brings about is a necessity. This type of thinking had a great influence on Jacques Derrida (1930-2004) and post-modern philosophy in general. In a conference given in Kassel (Germany) Derrida asked himself 'Can I die?', 'Is my death possible?' Obviously, he was not questioning the fact that at some point a living creature will die. The question was quite different: Can I die? Can death 'happen' to me? Do I experience my own end? Can I meet my own death? Derrida tried to deconstruct the life/death dualism to prove that it actually leads to an aporia (a logical discontinuity, an absurdity). There is a disconnection between logic and material reality.

Derrida is saying that I cannot meet my death because for there to be an 'I' there must be life, so death is an impossibility while there is life. And yet we die. Death is a limit of thought, because it is not representable. Death is an aporia because on the one hand it is something objective but on the other hand it is something unreal for the subject who dies. It is a certainty, but a certainty that it is impossible to represent.

In an interview in The New York Time Magazine Derrida confessed that:

'All my writing is on death. If I don't reach the place where I can be reconciled with death, then I have failed. If I have one goal, it is to accept death and dying.'

The future of death

As it is obvious to everyone, the subject of death (and what it means to us) is a topic that has concerned us throughout the ages and it will continue to do so in the future. In fact, one of the most exciting prospects for the next few years is the role that virtual and augmented reality, together with the metaverse, will play.

It is not inconceivable (and technologically we may not be that far off) that we could somehow defy our own mortality by creating a 'new reality'. If we manage to create avatars that are clones of ourselves, then biological death would reduce its destructive power. For this to happen our virtual clones will have the same physical features, accent, expressions, ideology, tastes, opinions and other personality traits. It would be a post-modern version of preserving the soul in the limbo of the metaverse once the body dies. Our relatives might be able to meet us on Christmas day or our birthday, even though we have passed away a long time ago. We might be able to have conversations, congratulate us, receive e-mails from us, remember anecdotes or introduce us to new family members, as long as we are in the metaverse or some other device that projects our interactive avatar. It could be that initially this will happen in a limited way becoming gradually more realistic over time. What is certain is that if we reach this point, a new type of ethical and legal situation will be generated and therefore we will face a new reality in which philosophy has a fertile ground.

Conclusion

There are very few things that can be done only once, but among them are being born and dying, unless one believes in reincarnation. Clearly, life and death are totally interconnected. If there is no death there could be no new life and vice-versa. Post-modern thought attempted to dismantle (deconstruct) the idea that they are two different entities. Instead, they are seen as two moments of the same existence. However, we need to understand this idea in a broader way, not as the mere existence of a particular individual. The life and death of individuals is part of a larger process of existence, but what that process might be is highly debated. Some believe that it responds to a divine plan, others that it is a cosmic law, some others that it is the evolutionary result of a universe born in the big-bang that latter evolved to create organisms that are constantly being born and dying as the best way to preserve life in a broader sense.

For thousands of years, death has been represented in a symbolic way because it is not easy to categorise it as a logical and rational idea. Most likely, life and death are not scientific terms but complex ideas full of connotations, whether they are moral, religious, social, legal, and any other.

As we have seen in the introduction, some live obsessed with the idea of death and others are constantly struggling to escape from it. However, more than death itself, what worries most people in our society is the limiting power that death has in their lives. One of our greatest fears is to experience a painful death, to a lethal disease that weakens us and prevents us from leading a normal life. In some countries euthanasia is legal to avoid precisely these situations. Death is considered to be a better option than a life that is slowly creeping to a painful end.

Being mindful of our finitude does not mean that we should constantly search for the elixir of eternal life. Nor does it imply living life as if we were corpses (think of Pelle Ohlin). Having death as a horizon can help us have a more adjusted vital project.

This is, of course, easier said than done. We all want to think of death as something far away that will happen to us when we reach old age after a long and fulfilling life with a golden retirement. However, we must be aware that this is not always the case and wars, accidents and incurable diseases can take us at an early age. Accepting that as part of our existence is another major challenge of our time.

EPILOGUE

The postmodern founders' patricidal work was great,
but patricide produces orphans
(David Foster Wallace)

About post-modern society and its individuals

Postmodern society is the result of a neoliberal capitalist mode of production. The combination of the market economy, digital technologies and globalization largely explain the emergence of this new society.

The fall of the Soviet Union and the transition from the communist bloc to free market economies have increased the expansion of post-modern societies.

The individuals that make up these new societies are obviously not all the same nor do they exactly fit a single definition. However, it is possible to give some general traits that would characterize post-modern individuals, even at the risk of caricaturing them. Furthermore, Western societies are not themselves fully post-modern. They are in a transition period that has not ended and that can be reversed at any time (wars, economic crises, pandemics, coups d'état, new scientific discoveries, technological advances, etc.)

However, if we had to describe a fully post-modern society, the greatest chances of victory belong to those who are not held down by strong roots. The post-modern individuals feel comfortable almost everywhere, but they don't belong anywhere. They have made instability and change their way of being and do not feel a strong attachment to any particular place. They are globalised individuals, unconcerned about the past or the future, always immersed in a changing present. This type of citizen always fly with the wind in their favour and swim with the current. They do not really care where it might take them, not least because they will not stay true to their destination for long. And this is not only applicable to the physical or geographical space they inhabit but also to their ethical, aesthetic and political thinking.

'Liquid individuals', or 'fragmented' or 'post-modern' (depending on the version that is preferred), do not necessarily have such strict and firm values, they can change them according to each situation. The same person can defend one thing and the opposite in a short period of time (when not simultaneously). What is right for them is what is most convenient. What is good is what works best in any given situation. As Groucho famously said: "These are mi principles and if you do not like them, I have others".

Political ideology is no longer a second skin, but rather an outfit that they change and alter according to the dress code of the event. The post-modernists' vote, their partners or even their style will change frequently, there are no loyalties that limit them. If necessary, they have no problem following the trends of the moment and then discarding them without any nostalgia. Tastes and long-term values disappear. It is a game of constant false starts and endings (which are also 'false' because nothing really ends, everything returns in some kind of revival as it is obvious in the fashion industry). It is a permanent flight forward.

In popular culture, the fragmentation we are referring to is quite obvious. In contemporary music, pigeonholing in a musical genre is seen as a limitation. There is no fusion or crossover of styles (as it might have been in the past), but a juxtaposition of genres. A post-modern song fragments, breaks, stops abruptly and starts again. Sounds dissolve and transform. The lyrics are not necessarily clear or coherent or use the same language. What at first seemed to be a jazz ballad in English becomes Spanish hip-hop and finishes with a church choir and electronic music.

Everything is dissolved and nothing is what it seems. Certainties disappear or are deconstructed. Relationships between people weaken or have a shorter duration in time (and intensity). Public institutions lose their authority and attractiveness (although not necessarily their power).

Every aspect of the post-modern society is taking on the characteristics of consumer goods in a market economy. Everything is bought and sold. Everything has an expiration date. Everything and everyone is susceptible of being improved and updated. To settle for what we already have is to lose. Even our body and our abilities are seen through this prism of constant updating and renovation (teeth, breast, nose, etc.). They are the equivalent of a human i-phone.

In this permanent flow, in this going from here to there without a fixed course or direction, necessarily the supreme good is 'freedom'. However, it is a freedom interpreted in a quite particular sense. Freedom is understood as being able to quickly change opinion, taste or position without being asked to account for it. The political, sexual or any other orientation can be changed without giving any explanations, it is enough to appeal to 'our freedom' to do so. It is just not anyone else's business.

The post-modern individual does not demand freedom to be something specific, instead they demand freedom to be nothing. Or rather, to constantly be something new, to be one thing today and another different tomorrow. There is an insistence in the idea of 'evolving', but without an ultimate purpose that guides and directs that evolution.

The past of the post-modern individual is not continuous and, like contemporary music, it is a juxtaposition of the past, a fragmentation of vital chapters, short episodes that do not point in any particular direction. The past is no longer an indicator of the future. In fact, in a post-modern society we should not talk about 'past' or 'future'. We should accept that there is a multiplicity of pasts and an infinity of simultaneous futures. There is no single present either, there are innumerable presents developing at the same time. This makes for a reality that is much more complex and difficult to analyse than in previous times. Of course, there were other presents developing simultaneously throughout History, however the dominant mentality in the past (the 'meta-narrative of power', in post-modern parlance) denied the existence or, at least, the validity of those alternatives. In more simple terms, the fiction created by those who are in power is called 'truth' and this truth represses any alternative that would question their authority. When the European arrived in America, their truth (Christianity) was the dominant one and could not admit the religion of the natives. However, post-modern individuals do not recognise any authority, they are the authority, and therefore individualism and free-market economies are so important for them.

Living in a post-modern society means that individuals are not one-dimensional, they are polyhedral instead, full of edges and contradictions. This is perceived as acceptable in the name of individual freedom.

Post-modern individuals generally don't mind sharing their intimacy. They are free from the fear of what others might think because nothing really defines or fully represents them. Today they can share some photos where they are looking after sick animals, tomorrow it is a black-tie party and a week later they share videos of an anti-capitalist demonstration they attended the day before they took a plane for an expensive vacation in Cuba. It is impossible to draw conclusions because any judgment would be false and contradictory. The post-modern individual is (and is not) many things at the same time. They are never trapped by their past because their past is so varied and incongruous that it unravels into chapters (or photos, audios or videos) of a present in constant flux.

However, it is very difficult to find individuals who are 100% post-modern. In fact, most of us are individuals in transition, not fully post-modern ones. In consequence we feel stressed, overwhelmed by the speed of events around us and the amount of information we have to handle.

The post-modern individual, is comfortable in the constant flow of the present. Perhaps it is the contemporary version of Nietzsche's 'super-man'[24]. They are not distressed when they see the expiration date on things, relationships or institutions. It is unlikely that fully post-modern individuals exist, yet their ghosts are constantly haunting us.

---

24. Nietzsche contrasts the super-man (*Übermensch*) with the degenerate last man of egalitarian modernity, an alternative goal which humanity might set for itself. An ideal for anyone who is creative and strong enough to master the whole spectrum of human potential, good and "evil", to become an "artist-tyrant". The *Übermensch* represents a shift from otherworldly Christian values and manifests the grounded human ideal.

Real or not, these fragmented individuals do not live attached to anything in particular and accept changes in their environment, in their work, in their family situation, etc. They are not merely stoic individuals who accept resignedly what fate brings them, post-modern individuals are also hedonists who enjoy the present, whatever it may be. They are both active and reactive, and move swiftly when they stop finding pleasure. In this sense, they lack a permanent place to rest.

For them, everything is debatable and open to interpretation. The limits are diffused and the borders are eliminated. Teachers, parents, doctors, scientists and any other figure of authority have a hard time understanding them. A fully post-modern individual might be a fiction, however, in Western capitalist societies we all have a varying percentage of post-modern sensibility in us.

The certainties of the past are not guarantees of anything in the present. Post-modernity questions any attempt at describing or defining people and things. What we used to believe to be indubitable is suddenly revealed to be unstable. And it is not simply about questioning some metaphysical issues such as the existence of God or the immortality of the soul. That has already been fully questioned and even ridiculed in modern philosophy. The great change of post-modernity manifests in the certainties of the individual. For example, it is questionable (or debatable) that I am 'a man'. It is true that I have male reproductive organs, but post-modernism asks what is 'a man' anyway? What does that mean? Is it just not being a woman? Why not allow more variability in the number of options? Why not completely remove the reference to gender?

Even certainties like 'nationality' are scrutinised under post-modern philosophy. Let's say that an individual is born in Germany and lives in Berlin for a large part of their life. Is this person German? What does it mean to be German? Are all Germans the same? Is there such a thing as 'the essence of Germany'? Everything that modern philosophy considered objective, in post-modern philosophy becomes subjective. Everything that supposedly defines us: gender, nationality, profession, social class, marital status, studies, etc. are called into question. In short, if you want to make a post-modern philosopher laugh, give them a definition of who you think you are.

SELECTED BIBLIOGRAPHY

Books

Allen, W., n.d. Apropos of nothing.

Aristóteles, P., 2011. Política. Madrid: Espasa.

Bauman, Z., 2017. Liquid times. Cambridge: Polity.

Bauman, Z. and Santos Mosquera, A., 2006. Vida líquida. Barcelona: Paidós.

Brennan, J., n.d. Against democracy.

Bueno, G., 2016. El mito de la cultura. Oviedo: Pentalfa.

Bueno, G., 2006. El mito de la izquierda. Barcelona, España: Zeta Bolsillo.

Bueno, G., 1996. El animal divino. 1st ed. Oviedo: Pentalfa.

Bueno, G., 1999. ¿Qué es la filosofía?. Oviedo: Pentalfa.

Butler, C., 2002. Postmodernism: A Very Short Introduction (Very short introductions). Oxford University Press.

Catullus, G., n.d. I hate and I love.

Concise Routledge encyclopedia of philosophy, 2000. London: Routledge.

Connor, S., 1997. Postmodernist culture. Oxford: B. Blackwell.

Copleston, F., 2003. A history of philosophy. London: Continuum.

Culler, J., 2002. Barthes. Oxford: Oxford University Press.

De Botton, A., 2014. The consolations of philosophy. London: Penguin Books.

Derrida, J., Brault, P., Kamuf, P. and Naas, M., n.d. Life death.

Derrida, J., 2000. Aporias. Stanford, Calif.: Stanford University Press.

Diamond, J., 2013. The world until yesterday. London: Allen Lane.

Drake, S., 2001. Galileo. Oxford: Oxford University Press.

Fisher, H., 2005. Por qué amamos. Madrid: Suma de Letras.

Fisher, M., 2010. Capitalist realism. Winchester, UK: Zero Books.

Foucault, M., Faubion, J. and Hurley, R., n.d. Power.

Foucault, M., 2013. Madness and Civilization. New York: Random House US.

Gutting, G., 2005. Foucault. Oxford: Oxford University Press.

Harris, J., 2006. The survivor. New York: Random House.

Harris, M., 1990. Cows, pigs, wars & witches. New York: Vintage Books.

Honderich, T., 2005. The Oxford companion to philosophy. Oxford: Oxford University Press.

Jameson, F. and Sánchez Usanos, D., 2012. El Postmodernismo revisado. Madrid: Abada.

Johnson, G., 2010. Renaissance art. New York: Sterling Pub.

Lovelock, J., 2016. Gaia : A New Look at Life on Earth. Oxford University Press.

Machiavelli, N., 2003. The prince. London: Penguin.

Magee, B., 1987. The great philosophers. London: BBC Books.

McWilliam, G., 2003. The Decameron. New York: Penguin Classics.

Moynihan, M. and Søderlind, D., 2003. Lords of chaos. Los Angeles: Feral House.

O'Donell, T., 2018. History of courtship. Skyhorse

Peeters, B., 2014. Derrida: A Biography. John Wiley & Sons.

Plat, García Gual, C., Martínez Hernández, M. and Lledó, E., n.d. Diálogos.

Plato, Candel, M. and Azcárate, P., 2011. La república o El estado. Madrid: Espasa.

Prideaux, S., n.d. I am dynamite! - a life of friedrich nietzsche.

Regan, T. and Singer, P., 1989. Animal rights and human obligations. Englewood Cliffs, N.J.: Prentice Hall.

Rousseau, J., 2003. A discourse on equality. London: Penguin.

Russell, B. and Tony Bruce., 2004. History of Western Philosophy (Routledge classics). Palgrave Macmillan Ltd.

Safranski, R. and Gabás, R., 2007. Un maestro en Alemania. Barcelona: Tusquets.

Safranski, R. and Gábás, R., 2019. Nietzsche. Barcelona: Tusquets.

Simon Glendinning., 2011. Derrida: a very short introduction. Oxford University Press.

Singer, P., 2015. Animal liberation. London: The Bodley Head.

Strathern, P., n.d. Death in Florence.

Taylor, V. and Winquist, C., 2001. Encyclopedia of postmodernism. London England: Routledge.

Trombley, S., 2012. Fifty thinkers who shaped the modern world. London: Atlantic.

Articles

Butler, J., n.d. Performative acts and gender constitution.

Moniz, A., 2013. Um olhar crítico sobre a saúde dos Rabelados de Espinho Branco. Revista de Ciencias da saude da ESSCPV, 5 (November 2013).

Stephens, M., 1994. Jacques Derrida. The New York Times, p.22.

The New York Times Magazine, 1996. Paco Can is canny; But is he art?. p.15.

Websites

En.wikipedia.org. n.d. Dead (musician) - Wikipedia. [online] Available at: <https://en.wikipedia.org/wiki/Dead_(musician)> [Accessed 21 June 2022].

Kreitner, R., 2016. Post-Truth and Its Consequences: What a 25-Year-Old Essay Tells Us About the Current Moment. [online] The Nation. Available at: <https://www.thenation.com/article/archive/post-truth-and-its-consequences-what-a-25-year-old-essay-tells-us-about-the-current-moment/> [Accessed 21 June 2022].

News.bbc.co.uk. 2004. BBC NEWS | Politics | UKIP candidate sparks gay anger. [online] Available at: <http://news.bbc.co.uk/1/hi/uk_politics/3666155.stm> [Accessed 21 June 2022].

News.bbc.co.uk. 2021. BBC NEWS / World/ Climate change: Young people very worried - survey. [online] Available at: https://www.bbc.co.uk/news/world-58549373

www.iranpresswatch.org. 2020. The 1980 Cultural Revolution and Restrictions on Academic Freedom in Iran. [online] Available at: <http://iranpresswatch.org/post/20819/1980-cultural-revolution-restrictions-academic-freedom-iran/> [Accessed 21 June 2022].

Tesich, S., 1992. A government of lies. - Free Online Library. [online] Thefreelibrary.com. Available at: <https://www.thefreelibrary.com/A+government+of+lies.-a011665982> [Accessed 21 June 2022].

Youtube.com. 2014. John MacArthur on Cal Tech and the Global Warming Hoax. [online] Available at: <https://www.youtube.com/watch?v=ZTlYl8E_B14> [Accessed 21 June 2022].